Poetry Ireland REVIEW 82

Eagarthóir/Editor

PETER SIRR

© Poetry Ireland Ltd 2005

Poetry Ireland Ltd/Éigse Éireann Teo gratefully acknowledges the assistance of The Arts Council/An Chomhairle Ealaíon and the Arts Council of Northern Ireland.

Poetry Ireland invites individuals and commercial organisations to become Friends of Poetry Ireland. For more details please contact:

Poetry Ireland Friends Scheme
Poetry Ireland
120 St Stephen's Green
Dublin 2
Ireland

or telephone +353 1 4789974; e-mail management@poetryireland.ie

PATRONS:
Joan and Joe McBreen

CORPORATE FRIENDS:
Bank of Ireland Arts Centre
ColourBooks Ltd
McEvoy Partners
Plus Print Ltd

Poetry Ireland Review is published quarterly by Poetry Ireland Ltd. The Editor enjoys complete autonomy in the choice of material published. The contents of this publication should not be taken to reflect either the views or the policy of the publishers.

ISBN: 1-902121-20-1
ISSN: 0332-2998

ASSISTANT EDITOR: Paul Lenehan with Rebecca L Curry
DESIGN: Alastair Keady (**www.hexhibit.com**)

Printed in Ireland by **ColourBooks Ltd** Baldoyle Industrial Estate Dublin 13

Contents   Poetry Ireland REVIEW 82

Thomas Kinsella

MARCUS AURELIUS

I   *On the Ego*

Gaspbegotten. In shockfuss.
          Out of nowhere.

Bent in blind sleep
          over a closed book.

Through the red neck
          cast out,

his first witness
          the gasp of loss,

to lie spent a while
          in the bloodstained shallows.

A little flesh. A little breath.
          And the mind governing.

II

Affairs were troubled in those days,
with over-confidence and ignorance everywhere.
A citizen, absent a while on an undertaking,
would find only increased coarseness on his return.

He himself, notable in his time and place,
and a major figure as later times would agree
(though for reasons that would have surprised his fellow citizens)
was in a false position:

                    cast in a main role,
while fitted with the instincts of an observer;
contending throughout his life with violent forces
that were to him mainly irrelevant.

Threatened on the Northern border by brutal tribes
with no settled homes – swift in the attack,
inspiring great fear; but ignorant and unskilled,
swift equally in the retreat –

these he dealt with, stemming their advance
and scattering them among their own confusions.
It was after his death that they resumed their incursions
that led to the break-up of the Western Empire.

A vaguer-seeming contagion out of the East,
more deadly in the longer term – in the citizens'
depths of will, and their dealings among themselves –
this he neglected.

                    Though it seems in retrospect
that nothing of any substance could have been done.
That it was irresistible
and in the movement and nature of things.

Called upon for decisive positive action,
at which he was more than averagely effective;
but preferring to spend his time in abstract inquiry,
for which he was essentially ungifted;

he kept a private journal, in Greek, for which
he is best remembered. Almost certainly
because it engaged so much of the baffled humane
in him, in his Imperial predicament:

accepting established notions of a cosmos
created and governed by a divine intelligence
– while pausing frequently to contemplate

the transient brutishness of earthly life,
our best experience of which concludes
with death, unaccountable and blank.

As to the early Christians, who might have helped
with their new simplicities, he took no interest,
unsystematic in their persecution,
permitting the martyrdoms to run their course.

III

Faustina, wife of Marcus, developed a passion
for a certain gladiator. She confessed this
to her husband, who had the gladiator killed
and his wife bathed in the blood. They lay together,
and she conceived and brought into the world
the son Commodus, who grew to rule
with Marcus for a while as Emperor,
and became sole ruler on Marcus's death
– coming to terms quickly with the Northern tribes.

His rule was arbitrary, bloody-minded,
centred on the Games; and culminated
in the belief that he was Hercules.
His plan to appear for an Imperial function
in the arena, dressed as a gladiator,
led to public outcry, and his assassination,
strangled in private among his close advisers.
His death, succeeded by chaos and civil war,
ended one of the Empire's longest periods
of civic affluence and stability.

– from *Marginal Economy*, to be published in The Peppercanister Series in 2005

Cherry Smyth

LONE WOLF LANGUAGE

In the land where she doesn't speak the tongue,
hers is quiet, lying less used,
except to eat, sing and lick her lips.
She likes living in silence in a thick coat,
where 'please', 'water' and 'thank you'
stand up like red roadside poles through deep snow.
The habits of the people are strange,
separate, but they understand a nod,
a pointing, a smile and money.
To look, learn, love and make a living –
she doesn't want much from the world,
just experience and time to write of it,
visit the shift between I and you and we,
words held with her teeth till the thaw.

ORPHEUS RIPPLE

While I was gone
you ran back into yourself
as water will when a glass has been
taken from and set back down

all bachelor
your body broke
regrouped in rapid time
to the skin of its own meniscus

my hair still wet
the face I had barely shown
pressed against your surface
mirroring itself

till my voice
surpassing muscularity and matter
dipped in through your glass
your silver and you let me sip

Cherry Smyth

BOG GOB

Gutter full of moss
a tongue where it shouldn't be
green language of rain.

NON-ATTACHMENT

The cloud is flayed
by the ridge of Slievemore
yet it does not rain.

ESTUARY

A mackerel sky
plays in the thinning water
as sand banks arise.

A wing of water
unfolds, fluttering over
the mirror of trees.

SUMMER

Writing rapidly
across the smooth white paper
amassing freckles.

Charles Wright

HERACLITEAN BACKWASH
 – for H V, fixed point in this flux

Wherever I am,
                    I always wonder what I am doing back there,
Strange flesh in a stranger land.
As though the world were a window and I a faint reflection
Returning my gaze
Wherever I looked, and whatever I looked upon.

Absence of sunlight, white water among the tall trees.
Nothing whispers its secret.
Silence, for some, is a kind of healing, it's said,
                            for others the end of a dark road
That begins the zone of a greater light.
Fish talk to the dead in the shallow water below the hill.

Or so the Egyptian thought,
                    who knew a thing or two about such things.
Strange flesh in a stranger land.
The clouds take their toll.
Like moist souls, they litter the sky on the way to where they're not.
Dandelions scatter across the earth,
                            fire points, small sunsqualls.

Biddy Jenkinson

'CROIDHE SEO Á GHOID UAINNE'
 — *Freagra ar dhán a scríobh, Mánas Ó Dónaill,*
  taoiseach Thír Chonaill i dtús an 16ú haois

Cuirim gairm scoile ort
i mbéal na Samhna is geimhreadh chugainn.
Bí ag filíocht im bhoth
seachas id chillín in aontumha.

Tabhair dom do chroí ar iasacht seal,
ón uair nach bhfuil croí agam féin.
 — Iasacht d'iasachta gheobhair uaim
gan a cochall léin. —

Gléasfad a fhéithe fada ceoil.
Goinfead iad le faobhar
go gcaoinfir i ndíle mire cordaí
dubhaigéan

a sheolfair ar thromthéada suain
go seinnfead goileog ghéar
is go n-éireoir chun rince ar
achainí mo mhéar.

Óir níl dubh nach nglacfaidh gile
le taitneamh gréine,
cláirseach nach rachaidh sna cranna ceoil
má labhraíonn céis.

Tabhair dom iasacht de do chroí
ón uair go bhfuil dhá chroí id chléibh
nó seol mo chroí féin chugam ar ais
go scoil an léin.

Alan Jude Moore

THE FOUNTAIN
 – *after St Patrick's*

People return their library books conscientiously
on Saturday morning. I don't know where I am.

A fountain in Eyre Square spews green water,
as if it was meant to. As if you might even believe it.

Although used to blatant displays of this nature,
it still upsets you. Read on a wall, 'BEAUTY

IS ON THE INSIDE'. The small print unclear.

Like a foreigner, or a spy, I conspire to spot my own kind.
Neither of us really care. Or say anything much about it.
(At least here they know how to contain a shopping centre).

Like any illegal worth his salt, found a good dark end
at the bar, just light enough to establish
the girls are pretty sitting on the wounded knee of America.

Lost off High Street, the optimism of a small city strikes me
when the sunrise and Hare Krishna chants collide.

I can still say only what I am not. Mumbling Montale,
that one phrase in Italian. Like any good forgetful night,

find a friend who talks more than you. Even *as Gaeilge*;
you can pretend to listen. You might even believe it yourself,

when you tell people if you lived where they did
you would also return your library books on time,

not read the small print; optimistically watch the sunrise
                              drown itself in green.

– reprinted from *Black State Cars* (Salmon Poetry, 2004)

Alan Jude Moore

ZAGORSK

She sits and says a prayer in the morning
that she takes another step back from the ledge
and the birds outside on the electrical wire
sing like the choirs at Zagorsk.
She stands by the window and says it's Spring.
Minus nine might turn to minus five.
She picks the right boots to wear
and ties her hair into an Imperial style.
This weather is not for everyone.
The Empire is frozen and the apartments are cold.
The birds outside on the electrical wire
pick at the air waiting for grass to grow.

Margaret Atwood

MOURNING FOR CATS

We get too sentimental
over dead animals.
We turn maudlin.
But only those with fur,
only those who look like us,
at least a little.

Those with big eyes,
eyes that face front.
Those with smallish noses
or modest beaks.

No one laments a spider.
Nor a crab.
Hookworms rate no wailing.
Fish neither.
Baby seals make the grade,
and dogs, and sometimes owls.
Cats almost always.

Do we think they are like dead children?
Do we think they are part of us,
our animal soul
stashed somewhere near the heart,
fuzzy and trusting,
and vital and on the prowl,
and brutal towards other forms of life,
and happy most of the time,
and also stupid?

(Why almost always cats? Why do dead cats
call up such ludicrous tears?
Why such deep mourning?
Because we can no longer
see in the dark without them?
Because we're cold

without their fur? Because we've lost
our hidden second skin,
the one we'd change into
when we wanted to have fun,
when we wanted to kill things
without a second thought,
when we wanted to shed the dull grey weight
of being human?)

STRING TAIL

I used to have helpfulness tacked onto me
like a fake string tail on a mangled dog.
Wag, wag, wag, went my nerveless appendage:
If I give you something, will you like me?

Watch me make you happy!
Here's a dry stick for you!
I fetched it off the ash heap.
Here's a dead bird.
There! Aren't I good?

Here's a gnawed bone,
it's my own,
I took it out of my arm.
Here's my heart, in a little pile of vomit.

Was it my fault you were angered
by the world news? That you badmouthed God
and banking, and also the weather?
That you sulked all day and were vicious
to your mirror, and also
to the girls at checkout counters?
That you thought sex was a mess?

I did my best. Wag, wag,
went my tail of string.
Have some drool and mud!
Admire my goodwill! It clings
to the soles of your boots
like soft pink melting jelly.

Here, take it with you!
Take everything, and then I'm free;
I can run away. I'm blameless.
You can have the string tail, too.

THE POETS HANG ON

The poets hang on.
It's hard to get rid of them,
though lord knows it's been tried.
We pass them on the road
standing there with their begging bowls,
an ancient custom.
Nothing in those now
but dried flies and bad pennies.
They stare straight ahead.
Are they dead, or what?
Yet they have the irritating look
of those who know more than we do.

More of what?
What is it they claim to know?
Spit it out, we hiss at them.
Say it plain!
If you try for a simple answer,
that's when they pretend to be crazy,
or else drunk, or else poor.
They put those costumes on
some time ago,
those black sweaters, those tatters;
now they can't get them off.
And they're having trouble with their teeth.
That's one of their burdens.
They could use some dental work.

They're having trouble with their wings, as well.
We're not getting much from them
in the flight department these days.
No more soaring, no radiance,
no skylarking.
What the hell are they paid for?

(Suppose they are paid).
They can't get off the ground,
them and their muddy feathers.
If they fly, it's downwards.
into the damp grey earth.

Go away, we say –
and take your boring sadness.
You're not wanted here.
You've forgotten how to tell us
how sublime we are.
How love is the answer:
we always liked that one.
You've forgotten how to kiss up.
You're not wise any more.
You've lost your splendour.

But the poets hang on.
They're nothing if not tenacious.
They can't sing, they can't fly.
They only hop and croak
and bash themselves against the air
as if in cages,
and tell the odd tired joke.
When asked about it, they say
they speak what they must.
Cripes, they're pretentious.

They know something, though.
They do know something,
something they're whispering,
something we can't quite hear.
Is it about sex?
Is it about dust?
Is it about fear?

Margaret Atwood featured in this year's Poetry Now Festival in Dún Laoghaire

C K Williams

COWS

Face in her hands, bike
thrown down beside her, a girl
on the road from the village
stands broken-heartedly crying.

I assume it's some little love-
thing but stop a ways on
to be sure; in a meadow nearby,
ten or so spotted heifers,

each with a numbered tag
in her ear, see me and rush
to the fence and low over,
all of them, all at once,

with so much feeling that not
'Feed me!' do they seem
to be saying but 'Save me!'
Save me! Save me! Save me!

Still long-legged,
still svelte, their snug
skin milk-white
and gleaming, obsidian black...

I think of Io, transformed
by treacherous Zeus to a heifer,
whose beauty was still such
men longed to embrace her.

These, by next year, unless
they're taken to slaughter,
will be middle-aged ladies
with udders, indifferently grazing.

When I look in the mirror, the girl –
should I have offered to help her? –
is gone: I'll never know what
happened to her, nor what will.

The cows watch still,
jaws grinding, tails lashing
the squadrons of flies on their flanks.
Save me! Save me!

C K Williams featured in this year's **Poetry Now Festival** in Dún Laoghaire

Eamon Grennan

DREAMING IN TUSCANY

It's the open cornflowers and the Queen Anne's lace
burning their own particular blue and white
beside the railway line (in tawny fields from which
the grass or wheat or rye has been already harvested),

as well as the blazing acres of sunflowers showing
their brilliant faces to the clouded sky the sun is
hiding behind, which put a stop to the swallow-stab
of question after question slitting my dream-unsettled

head to bits and no answering. Was the funeral
I found myself at a cover for something? Whose
hand was I supposed to shake in sympathy, whose
eyes to keep at bay? Nothing could be explained:

two countries running into one, a couple of continents
dissolved into the single small space where someone
was to be buried and there's scarcely room to breathe.
I have heart only to stay on guard, unable to do anything

except refuse to believe in any of these absolutes but
to go on looking, asking discreet questions, searching
faces. Final as it is, this funeral isn't the last word
on the subject, and by the time the train is taking me

south – past fields of sunflowers candescent after rain –
I have to settle myself among my daylight family, let
slip the dream-leash, knowing always there are more
where that one came from and they'll find me.

Eamon Grennan

STEAM

It could be the glide and slide of traffic
over wet streets – funereal, with headlights on –
or some more minute distraction, looking
for the woodpecker on the bare branch: brief
handful of feathers, scarlet head, incorrigible beak.

Or seeing in this frigid February morning,
the brief love affair that great burst of steam
as it funnels from the power house valve
and explodes in a huge bloom of cloud
has with the February air.

Brevity! Brevity! the heart cries
at that whole rolling mass melting in no time
to a few white wisps
curling away: nothing to them – yet
brighter than anything in the grey morning
their dying glitter.

Gerry Murphy

A THOUSAND PAGES FROM THE BOOK OF LONGING
 – for M M

Do you remember the cat
in Winthrop Street?
It was calm in my arms,
a warm throbbing bundle
steeped in the late colours of autumn.
Do you remember
the first hint of winter,
the Earth already swinging out
to the coldest arc of its orbit,
its chilled flame rising
to your earlobes
your ivory earlobes
your earlobes of brilliant marble
your earlobes of a lake's edge
in moonlight
your earlobes of glistening wax
in an abandoned cathedral
your pearl earlobes
your emerald earlobes
your earlobes of snow
your earlobes of the belly
of the orchid
your earlobes of the bowels
of the rose
your neon earlobes
streaking across the glass-grey evening
towards the moon
your ozone oh your ozone earlobes
swirling within that blue blue hemisphere
the roof of your mouth around the dream red
sun red dream the tip of your tongue
your earlobes of incredible opulent splendour
opening into the high vaulted caverns
of your ears
inside all would be beryl
and opal and sapphire and sardonyx
and pure gold
outside the black flag of anarchy
floating on a melancholy breeze.

Eugene McCabe

WHAT A PIECE OF WORK IS MAN

I was six. The squeal came from our turf shed
Where the walls were catacombed with rat runs.
Afraid to see it caged I called for Ned
Hackett who could ring bulls and graip tons
Of dung on spud ground from a moving sled
And fierce proud to hail from Ballindarcy.
'Itself did you see him caught?' 'No,' I said.
'Rats are bad buggers,' he said, 'no mercy
For that boyo, alive we'll roast the thief.
You fetch papers lad, I'll get twigs of beech.
They'll quit their thieving when they hear his grief.'
The cage held over flames, that sickening screech,
My father running with a shouted curse –
'Christ rats are bad but man you're ten times worse!'

Susan Wicks

DREAM

You only had to leave and your bedroom
has rolled out into space
in a swirl of branches where the full moon
presses its pale face to the glass.
There's a pool of milk under the sill.
I'm paddling in white blood
that dries without a trace. A trail
leads from the curtain to the made bed

where something of you still lies
looking up at these posters – a man on his knees
slick as a seal in his blue latex sheath;
a ripple of ochre desert; a gold-silk-trousered Puck
pinned in mid-leap with a message: *Back
in forty minutes*; the spinning earth.

Susan Wicks

3 A.M.

I wake to a jolt
of something like shame,
the mattress under my spine
pulsing heat,
the sweat
a seethe of ants under my skin

as if in a dream
my body itself
were trying to relive
the mistakes of years.

I throw back the quilt
and air laps me awake,
flows over my face
my fingers, my spread thighs,
my slowing heart.

I think of cold
clean things, frost
feathering the white ground,
the cars parked nose to tail
on the street outside,
their windscreens furred,
the wiper blades iced hard

and I curl in
to your smooth back
that is still itself
and smells of skin
and cotton, chlorine, tarka dhal
and luck.

Naomi Foyle

3 POEMS FROM 'THE ONLY GHOST I EVER SAW I THOUGHT WAS YOU'
  – i.m. Mairtín Crawford, 1967-2004

SPACE

You were known
for being obsessed with space

writing poems about UFOs,
Moonmen, Mir and Jupiter

scoring an arts grant
to photograph NASA

sitting in the cockpit
of rockets

worrying about asteroids
falling from the sky.

I read your cover story
– Belfast astronomers on red alert –

foolishly believed myself
a little safer on the earth.

WRONG END OF THE TELESCOPE

Little details always gave you pleasure.
Snails on the cliffs at Whitehead,
crawling up.
Signature phrases:
Easy peasy lemon squeezy.
Okey doke.
Bok choi in the fridge.
Toto: 'She's a Pomeranian, you know.'
That Muldoon poem about trees
you read to me three times
perched on the edge of the bed.

Small things also enraged you.
Perceived slights.
Accidental brushes with indignity.
Dog shit
on your coat
before the Ulster-Scots debate.

I learned not to laugh.

If you had tunnel vision
it was a mountain shaft on fire.

LEAVING BELFAST
  April 2004

After three months of mourning
after going under and re-emerging
after reading that Muldoon poem
'Wind and Tree'
to a festival hall full of people who loved you,
carrying your notebooks, old school essays,
diary entries, NASA research
strapped to my body
like a lifejacket
or a bomb,
the trust of your mother
wrapped up in my promise
to decipher your handwriting
gather your poems together –
I find myself weeping
from one eye
in the airport lounge
on the plane
and on the train.
For the next three days
back in Brighton
my left eye overflows
with clear water,
tears oozing one by one
like snails upon my cheek.
Did you get caught in a draught?

my landlady asks.
Yes, the door
between winter and spring
was open a crack.
A cold, sharp wind
drove me back up the Lisburn Road
to pick up my luggage
and call for the taxi
to take me away
from the people you loved
the place where you lived.

Wislawa Szymborska

PORTRAIT OF A WOMAN

She must come in many varieties.
To change so that nothing ever changes.
It's easy, impossible, hard, worth trying.
Her eyes are, as needed, now deep blue, now grey,
dark, playful, brimming for no reason with tears.
She sleeps with him like a one-night stand, like his one and only.
With him, she will have four children, no children, one.
Naïve, yet giving the best advice.
Weak, yet able to bear anything.
Has no head on her shoulders, but will have.
Reads Jaspers and ladies magazines.
Doesn't know what this screw is for and will build a bridge.
Young, as usual young, as always still young.
Holds in her hands a little sparrow with a broken wing,
her own money for a journey long and distant
a meat-cleaver, a poultice and a shot of vodka.
Where is she running like that, isn't she tired?
Not at all, just a bit, very much, it's not a problem.
Either she loves him or is determined to.
For better, for worse, and for heavens sake.

– translated by **Justyn Hunia** and **Alice Lyons**

Tom Mac Intyre

ENCOUNTERING ZOE

I
Avoid the unforced error,
honeyed *faux pas*, of asking
the former, decades later, to send,
if no trouble, some shots of your
time together, scarcely a word exchanged
since, so what, people meet, hills don't,
she will respond –

            And then some.
The envelope arrives, lightweight,
such restraint, *she* doesn't figure,
of the handful one matters, one
jumps the years, life to come.
It's a shot, the hand pales,
of you, happiest man by far
in the ring of Ireland, shot
taken, early seventies, by a genius
Russian poet who died young, it shows:
the subject – backdrop of rocks, ocean –
is haunted, and in love; better,
haunted *by* love, that rare –
(comparatively) condition, ter-
minal, sure, they're working on it,
I believe –

            Grab time out. Phone
to say thanks, mention (*de rigeur*)
your stake in that particular shot,
cock the starveling bothered ear.
It harvests intake-of-breath-cum-
sibilant, tapering, beyond analysis –
O, bagel-baby of my salad days, O,
lax and gefilte-fish of lazy Sabbath noon –
we two made a view of islands,
lighthouse beam, we made more,
there was a garden took the eye,

her, a wonder, carrying our mite
the few brave months – and gone –

2
April scantling, dim quiet after
in which purrs *maxima culpa*,
did you sufficiently delight,
do you, will you, some day, never,
give blood to the wishing-well?

25 today, Finger-Lake District,
New York State, she's thinly clad,
cool buzz back of her inaud-
ible, encyclical, mastic: she
explains, daughter Zoe's Conferring,
an occasion, few friends around,
Zoe's, theirs. . . Yes. That time of year,
Latinate scroll, decked, ribbon –
bound, reach, let your hand
touch, caress, the furled oblong,
Zoe, dear near-relation, *Sé
do bheatha, Zoe*. I bow to a mother,
to a daughter fair, retreat
to the shades where I belong.

Louise C Callaghan

SOULCASE
  – for Lara

In the framer's workshop, the basement,
we stood among frames stacked against every wall,
paintings on canvas, on board behind glass.
I talked out my latest business,
while you two waited all eyes.

After the crazy street the air, cold as a morgue.
You pulled your little brother in to see,
tucked behind layers three deep,
a small box-frame picture
containing a baby's woollen cardigan.

Pinned like a butterfly.
Too small for a new-born,
not worn more than once or twice,
then washed too hot. It was perfect:
a tiny rosebud motif near each shoulder seam,

knotted in a green leaf. Purl/plain, purl/plain:
the ripple of wool through learning hands.
Neither of you spoke a word
as if remembering your infant sister.
Her airless coffin settled on the mountain-side.

John O'Donnell

THE WAVE

– in memory of those who perished in the Fastnet Yacht Race, 1979

Grizzled mainsail trimmer off a Yankee clipper
the only one to call it, cloudless August morning
in the shore-side caff. 'Something big

out there in the Atlantic,' southern drawl amid
Sweet Afton, waft of last night's beer, bitching
about skippers over eggs and bacon. Tinkling

masts. The gleam and spank of sail, yachts prancing
in the harbour, courses plotted for The Rock. No runic
satellite, no merry weather-man could then foretell

the mangled spars. The drifting empty hulls.
The sodden bodies hauled aboard by trawlers;
the others, never found, lists taped up in windows

near the greasy spoon where that old salt had seen
what Hokusai saw, beyond the geishas and the fishmarkets
of Edo, his own floating world as he leaned over

a wood-block carved from cherry to make his picture
of the wave off Kanagawa: out of nowhere, a rumble
in the ocean, foam-flecked surge gathering in the arc

of its own rage into a roar of water, brute beauty
trembling above the wooden sampans, the cowering men.
Poised. Ready to sweep everything away.

Mike Shields

HERE AND THERE, NOW AND THEN
  – Stirling, Scotland; Mizen Head, Ireland
        . . .and whether he loves me, or loves me not
        I will walk with my love now and then. (Irish, Traditional)

There, on the high cliff
in July mist,
disturbed by all the signals
calling me
the steel sun
the white sky
the wild Atlantic
innocent as aluminium foil
in the vast west-light,
I look, intent, intensely
as if by wish alone
I could translate
through all that intervening air
to where you are.

Here, the land is lush
for late September,
green and grey the colours now
grey of sky, of water
feeding the late leaves
the still-growing grass
filling the little loch
green of grass, of leaves and weeds
living, strangely, for
(as you would call it) fall
is drifting down the hillsides
in the dying heather
and winter waits behind the Highlands
in the territories of frost.

Then, the sun's bequest
was luscious Ireland
as we walked the path,
the hill like some soft green fruit
sliced through,

the afternoon abuzz
with insect conversations,
and we meeting only
through telegraphs of thought,
molecules of air
Marconi-like
linking continents.

Now, over the green,
boys are playing soccer in the orange afternoon;
too early, really, for the winter game
but sounds recall for me a time
of leather-smells and wet leaves
ball slapping into waiting hands,
muddy cheers.
Too many autumns (you have noted)
gone since then
too many helicopter leaves
too many Dylan birthdays
making me aware how long the shadows are
how cold the wind is
when it whistles time.

Mostly, faith is the assumption that
the universe is not
the pastime and the jest
of some sadistic autocrat
who places gifts past finger-reach,
gives half a talent,
links us by love, yet makes us live
a continent apart.
And so, my dear, we must be content
to be long-distance lovers
neither innocent nor guilty,
damned to meet in dreams
walk by the rivers of your poems
communicate by remote imagination
here and there,
now and then.

Declan Collinge

ATHBHREITHNIÚ STAIRE

Scríobann an cloíteoir fírinne scriosta
Na staire ó línte catha morálta
A ghabhtar le linn bua.

Airíonn an tainniseoir
Pian abhreith fírinne,
Curtha ó rath, maolaithe as riocht.

Ní fhaightear id mhiontuairiscí mé,
Gan teideal agam ar d'uaireanta
Ár ndála mar uimhreacha neamhscríofa.

Sula dtugann tú faoi athbhreithniú
Meabhraigh an croí a tairgeadh,
Nó cumhracht doimhin an phaisin

A chuir ar meisce ár gceadfaí,
Beir beo ansin ar do pheann
Agus scrios go hiomlán mé.

Declan Collinge

AISTEAR TRAENACH

'Buaileann an Bás síos bóthar
Córóin de bhlátha oráiste dreoite uirthi.'
   – Federico Garcia Lorca

I dtromluí doiléir, suím
Ar bord traenach, dord miotalach
Na rothaí dom chiapadh,
Imeachtaí mo shaoil ag scinneadh
Tharam sna fuinneoga,
Corrán géar na gealaí
Ag bagairt orm ón spéir.

Meabhraím aistear traenach
Ó Mhadrid go Valencia na Spáinne,
Spréachadh agam ar radharc tíre
Donn faoi scalladh gréine;
Mothaím fós teas millteanach
An lae dom imchlúdach,
An tallas tríom amach.

Scuabtar an dá aistear le chéile
Mar a scuabtar duilleoga
Le fuadar tuarúil stoirme,
Baill chorp agus bagáiste
Á séideadh le fórsa ar ardán
Ár nuaire agus ceist fós dom chiapadh
An é an tromluí an saol?

Gary Allen

EXPLOSION

Hoops of rusted wire will make a mesh
for wet concrete

like giant lobster creels
or eel baskets

they wait under the pale blue sky
and are bait as well as trap

for what is living, or manmade:

here in the pipe-yard the dust and fine cement
will blow across the leviathan sheds

clog sluices, crankshafts, iron teeth

and the grey faced ghosts from Charon's boat,
dull pennies in their mouths,

will come out into the sunlight and stare.

The first one speaks without words
that he shouldn't have been there

but was caught between blast and heat
that seared all hair from the body

fused bone in its intensity

as the backbone of a fish
will peel away from the flesh

another shrugs, it is the brightness
the fragility of metal,

the third smells faeces.

And in one voice they sing
through the strange hollows,

It doesn't matter
for we were nothing worth destroying
in such a way.

Gerard Smyth

ECCLES STREET

It was the silver age of the sepia print.
From Eccles Street
the wanderer set out in the heat of June,
to take the epic route,

to make a day of small detours
with cronies in the meeting rooms
and hostelries.
Journey-man. Pilgrim. Tenant
of a creaky house

that after slow decline was gone in time,
I retrace your path
from the precinct of the dispossessed
to the dunes in Sandymount

and the round Martello with its climbing
steps and assonant echoes
that echo still, a hundred years since
Odysseus prowled his Dublin streets
and bawdy-house.

Hugh O'Donnell

WHENEVER

It must have been before they invented waiting lists
for a go on the machines
or contrived a moon walk with sponsored astronauts
advertising away from home

and we could have spared ourselves the hullabaloo
that followed as the usual
caught up with us again – the body presenting itself
each morning for inspection

while making long-term plans for the imminent return
of you-know-who with his mop
(and bucket), flicking over the spilt milk of our lives;
hardly a backlash, hardly 'I told you so.'

John Montague

THE HAG'S COVE

Over the steeped, heaped seaweed
the flies, shimmering blue-black
and gold, sing their song of harvesting,
of dissolution, the necessary process
of putrefaction, decay's deadly drone.

Thick dragons' tails of wrack,
frilled flutter of dulse,
a song of things breaking down,
other things feeding upon them,
a compost heap of dissolving forms,
a psalm, a threnody of decomposition.

I made my way there, daily,
a sort of dark pilgrimage,
mind and body freshening
after the habitual soilings,
(tensions of work, family,
ceaseless sour quarrels),
soothed by the ocean's
eternal turning flange,
its vast devouring indifference,
blue and calm, or bruised and folding
with angry, heaving motion.

Along the promontory
stand three stone towers,
not only 'dead at the top'
but hollowed, useless, except
as a sanctuary for wild animals,
for nestling birds, or lovers
fleeing the constant coastal rains.

Such a long time since compass,
spyglass and binoculars
watched and waited for
the great Atlantic liners,
Cunard and White Star,

carrying their cargo of pain away
(torn families, old-fashioned exile tears)
or, laden with success, returning
(the glossy suit of the prodigal son):
looming shapes at the mouth
of Cork's verdant, unfurling harbour.

One smashed down here, below,
a Captain drunk in his bunk
as his charge rammed the rocks;
caught and tossed all day
between the Cow and the Calf,
Slowly smashed into smithereens;
now a hushed pub legend.

To allow oneself to be swallowed again,
repossessed by nature's thick sweetness
(Over the steeped, heaped seaweed
the flies sing their song of harvesting),
that hectic glitter of decay,
that gluttonous moil of creation,
to be smashed on the rocks,
broken down and built again,
clutching at the intimate softness
of tough reed, brave flower,
swaying at the cliff's edge,
like the mind on its fraying tether;
What shall we do with *this drunken sailor*
early in the morning?

– reprinted from *Drunken Sailor* (Gallery Press, 2004)

John Montague featured in this year's **Poetry Now Festival** in Dún Laoghaire

Peter Robinson

from THERE ARE AVENUES

Across buckled asphalt, past rows of lamps,
by Springwood Crem my father drives.
Under a sky-full of copper beech leaves'
congealed blood colour, his blue car goes.
It's been a good August for funeral fees.
They're not deducted from his stipend
since retiring: he's flush at summer's end.
White memorials glint through trees.

Then Banks Road's seen in late evening sun,
bright, down at the horizon
with a quarter moon here in broad daylight;
it brings back uncalled-for memories
now to this long wall curving beyond
Garston's surviving gasholder,
here to the churchyard, and this way
the vicar would take on his rounds
as he drives you back once more –
both trespassing, as it were,
across the bounds of his successor.

Under the Bridge and towards the docks,
seen in a late evening sun you go
driven towards a memory's places
where things haven't changed that much despite
the water flowed under this bridge,
timber ships stopped, and other things gone
on that gap-toothed or toothless horizon –
like the bobbin works long derelict,
Bryant & Mays closed down
or the aerodrome, for one more instance,
turned to a luxury business hotel
with Dragon Rapide parked at its forecourt
(the first plane we ever went up in
on a joy ride one summer at Southport).

Through the false dawns and declines
things haven't changed that much, you see;

you see faces peering from street doors
or pressed to a sweet shop's bleached display;
you hear a poor child's unconsoled crying
again, and as if that weren't enough
they're spending money like a man with no hands,
EU money on futuristic street lamps
for the shopping-precinct's dual carriageway.

*

That Sunday morning, one July, we went
to fritter the time and slake a thirst
past haciendas, dream bungalows
with families' cars parked outside in rows
down Quarry Street where property values
fell with the land to industrial cottages –
as if this hill represented the stages
of the whole class system's rise and fall.

Climbing or descending, we'd seen it all –
from converted farm's swimming pool
to outside loos… Here, public school rebels
would play uneasy games of darts
with regulars, deal out hands of Hearts
in a backroom at the Cobden Vaults…
And though there's a good ten years between us,
these pauses in our talk must mean
that even for you change comes
to incumbents of pubs, their altered names,
saloon bars refurbished with imported brands.

Further, the sock and stocking factory stands
with broken glass panes, silent, still,
in a hollow half-concealed by the steep curve of its hill.
Then a car with first-time buyers arrives
as we hang around waiting for the locals to open.
This place had once seemed stratified, confined.
Now jammed against striated red sandstone,
the disused quarry, are starter homes –
some raw earth for their gardens…

As you say, I'll just go for a walk and write about it;
but you know I got into that habit

when we were still living in the vicarage
with its quarrels and silences, its differences of age;
and then I'd have to get out of the house,
walk off those feelings, make sense I suppose,
come home in the small hours, or sometimes next day,
barely relieved of an urge to get away
as I ran from myself at one o'clock or two
down Brodie, or Mather, or Menlove Avenue.

*

Like a case of mistaken identity,
tell me about it, tell me
about how it feels being on your way home
underneath a cherry-tree row
only yards from the house round the corner
as you look up to find yourself lost
in unrecognized places, one more time –
and police sirens sound down the boulevard;
you're lost before things in themselves.

So it must have been after that lift
dad gave me to the Post Office.
I was sending word to this side of the world
by surface mail or swift-air…
'Look at them,' I said, birds' nests in high branches
of Booker Avenue's pre-spring trees
like knots in tangled hair.

'Up there, out of touch,' he said,
'like you say you like to be.'
But as he did, in weakening eyes,
whether out of touch or not
along Brodie Avenue's verges and islands
from front garden walls birds dropped
down to their worm-filled ground.

Fenced around by municipal railings
the monolith's blotched with lichen;
it stands lost in a grove of privet,
its niche one generous bite
taken from somebody's manicured lawn.
Gouged grooves, shallow graffiti

had stopped you, dazed by a recent arrival,
stepping back here to remember who you are.

Then like a worn-smooth gravestone,
those meaning marks of sacrificial worship
from the remote, raw centuries
would make time disappear –
as again I'm glimpsing bits of landscapes
where suddenly shapes
of dead friends' faces come to mind
under the fruiting cherry trees.

It's as if everyone in particular
had carried me off from a late July's
sun-flecked street and I float with the hours
past so many ranged in the open
at pub tables, near parked cars
or mooching along quite on their own
by a bungalow with its flag unfurled –
everyone focal to themselves
at home, or it seems so, in this world
of unclouded suburb skies.

*

On that same road between cemeteries
this far north in our hemisphere,
an after-supper evening sun
flares once more through the copper beech trees'
red-black leaves; they're semi-transparent
above costly marble where someone
walks acres solid with bereavement.
Shadows fatten round hedges near,
hedges entangled with convolvulus trumpets
and, involved, a couple pass
just like they don't notice.

From two late trains, it's come to this.
Sun splotches in the heart-shaped leaves
disarm me as they push back recent
instances of headlamp beams
that dazzled but quickly moved on
past faces caught in pub-door laughter

at gossip, delicious opinion –
hopes come to this years or moments after
now that evening's late light rains
down through these clotted-blood-colour leaves
picking out their splayed veins.

But like so many childhood scabs,
those meanings just evaporate
here in the silence of now –
this posthumous sensation, this late
feeling I should have foreseen;
and, yes, it's like the slabs
that glint through privets, shrubs, and trees
had petrified our angry words,
translated, buried them
in such overcrowded ground.

Beyond foreseeable disappointments
not to be written off, you remember,
at one with other equivocal things
like the children who've turned into parents,
or a sixty-year-old concrete pillbox
abandoned behind black railings…
But as traffic lights turn amber
in timely warmth, why not relax
now dusk suffuses empty sky
and kids at play on a churchyard wall
have no earthly reason to recall
anybody else going by?

Lavinia Greenlaw

CAMEL HAIR

Every few years it becomes
a question of backbone.

Anhedonia,
not love of winter

but a loss of the feel of the world,
a way ahead of the cold.

Even the cells refuse
to talk to one another.

As black and white
as a two-hour wait on the kerb

of a six-lane arterial road,
in a secondhand straw-coloured Dior coat,

for the last bus and its overload
to accelerate past out of its own

well-oiled backsplash.

– reprinted from *Minsk* (Faber, 2003)

Lavinia Greenlaw featured in this year's **Poetry Now Festival** in Dún Laoghaire

Aifric Mac Aodha

ATHAIR AGUS INÍON

X-AGUS O-ANNA

Ina suí dóibh sa charr,
Iad sáite sa tranglam,
Bhreacadar a n-eangacha
Ar cheochlár na gloine.
Ba rúndiamhair dise
I bhfiorthús a hóige
An tslí gur theip air
An líne a ghnóthú
'S gurb aicise an bua,
Gan dícheall, gan dua.

RÉALT

D'inis sé di gur thit
Réalt ón spéir anuas
Isteach sa phróca
A chóirigh sé
Ar thairseach
A fuinneoige.

Go fóill féin
Ní bhainfeadh sí
An barr de
Ar fhaitíos
Go n-éalódh
Orthu.

Olann

Mar bhlúirín uainolla
É i bhfostú i ndriseog:
Siúd mar a mhairfeadh
A ghrá di.

Aifric Mac Aodha

FATHER AND DAUGHTER

XS AND OS

Sitting in the car,
stopped in traffic,
they marked grids
on the fogged-up window,
it was a mystery to her
when she was very young
the way he failed to gain a row
the way she always, always won.

STAR

He told her
a star fell
from the sky
into the jar
he had placed
on her window-sill.

Even now,
she would not remove
the lid
for fear
it should escape
on them.

WOOL

Like a scrap of a lamb's wool
entangled in a briar:
so would survive
his love for her.

John Kinsella

THE OCEAN FORESTS: AN ELEGY AND LAMENT

As the gleam of growth
stills in harsh, cold sunlight,
and trees tap inner heat
through fibre-optics,
it starts to filter
through here – an earthquake
miles below the ocean's floor,
plate slipping under plate,
the massive release of energy
and surge of water
running the gradient
of landfall: forcing entry,
as deftly as fire, an elemental
crossover on the edge
of all that's living,
or catching sight
of where play or a conversation
rolls in the swell
uprooting the tree as body, as water
is the body we are, and when water
pulls back the soul escapes;
what do we see
in the whitewash,
the island wreckage,
the passing urge to push out
from the point of our disruption?
Calibrating prophecies
of the living, some look for signs
of punishment – there are none,
and those who want such outcomes
condemn us before we wake –
animals moved to higher ground.
Truth annuls our own disasters:
a local freeze or heatwave,
the light of the ocean forest
absorbed by warmer currents,
ice encasing an entire depth

at once pushed and drawn out,
swept with a rush to reshape,
supplant; this melding, curving,
heaving re-alignment. . .
the fulsome atmosphere
imprinted with cloud,
the seaweeds of new oceans,
new shorelines, haphazard burials,
an air pocket in a basement
as light and air saturate
wishful thinking, a choice
we make in a medium
of earth, water, air – no country
declares ownership in the bloom
of hot coral forests, ice forests
and memories of mimosa
from the driest parts.
We reflect from where we are,
where we were. The melting
and piercing of the earth's crust –
made viscous then fragile
then unstable? We search
for answers. We watch
sunsets with iridological
intensity, an emollition
of the planet's static,
a mirror stripped of its backing,
we stare up at the swimming,
the molten, the chilled, the drowning.
Cold and calculating:
rupture, megathrust. . .
absolving the apocalypse?
Language betrays disaster,
and makes culture
of the brutal fact: tsunami.
Twenty years ago
on the northern tip of Sumatra,
we reflected on direction:
the choices we might make.
Locals and visitors
brought together:

the warm winter-jaded
visitors linked over a meal
with those knowing each foot of ground,
grown fluid in the wobbling
of the earth's rotation,
shortening all our days,
bringing palm trees and ice forests
under the same cut-glass sky,
salt etching rock and wall
and metal strewn
about an epicentre,
boundaries of touch and impact,
lament and bubbles caught
on our face rising up to sight,
across the transparent divide
of blue fish and white birds,
infusion of haze
and light rebounding,
the swirl of those close
and lost already,
known even in the shock,
thoughts hovering where the body was,
is not. . .and we who know not how
to deal with others lost. . .
so this is all that will come out
of iced or burning forests?
How do we write: 'happy new year'
without the sharp
cut of water,
the burning wash?
How celebrate
seasons when winter
has reached down
into the warm,
torn shores of an ocean
so close, so distant. . .?

John Kinsella

OPPOSITE SIDES OF THE PADDOCK

They work opposite sides of the paddock,
cutting grass in the old way, older
than they ever knew, as old as their
grandparents' parents out in the sun;
they found their scythes separately,
at an auction, buried beneath tarps
up in the dead rat barn, collapsing now.
They curved the metal away from the body –
as suddenly cutting back to ghost
their limbs in the same measured stroke.
Looking up, distantly, to watch the other's
faint work, heat wavering over their shoulder.

John Kinsella

DRIVEWAY, YORK

NIGHT

The driveway at night –
The moon's yellow light –
Mice move quickly
Through brittle grass.
The driveway at night –
The moon's yellow light –
Cats and foxes overlap,
Move on briskly.
The driveway at night –
The moon's yellow light –
Gravel shifts underfoot,
Slip over dry watershed.
The driveway at night –
The moon's yellow light –
An easterly starts up,
Fence-wire vibrates.
The driveway at night –
The moon's yellow light –
Nightjar weirds you out,
Turn back to the house.

DAY

The driveway by day –
The sun's bright overlay –
Sixteenth-month-old Timothy
Making his way.
The driveway by day –
The sun's bright overlay –
Crows at right angles,
Galahs tearing it up.
The driveway by day –
The sun's bright overlay –
High ground walkway,
Valley a conversation point.

The driveway by day –
The sun's bright overlay –
Ants and their dead zones,
Places of transit and commerce.
The driveway by day –
The sun's bright overlay –
Jam trees and exfoliating granite,
Somewhere the golden whistler.

John Kinsella

AFTERWORD TO THE NEW ARCADIA

I have worked consciously on this volume – *The New Arcadia*, to be
published by Norton in 2005 – for four years, and probably unconsciously
for the twenty-five or so years that I've been trying to write a 'new'
pastoral, a pastoral that carries with it the ironies and contradictions of
any celebration of the rural, a mode of expression that recognises the
cultural inheritance as well as the cultural baggage of the bucolic.

The pastoral I have been writing is full of poison and celebration,
wheat and salinity, violence and the balminess of a post-harvest evening.
The neighbour riding his mower day in day out, cutting the same patch
of grass because he laments not working the big tractors any more, is a
source of wonder and irritation to me. He sprays poison over the
fenceline and has me vigorously protesting and defending our organic
lifestyle, though I've no doubt if you were in need he would be ready to
lend a hand no matter what. Nothing is straightforward – I never want to
write a poetry that says my way is the only way. *The New Arcadia* has
bitter poems, but they are as bitter about 'self' as about 'others.' I think I
move around among the voices – I don't think my 'character' is fixed
anywhere in particular. The anger and irritation are not necessarily, or at
least not always, my own!

Fundamentally, however, underlying the work is a recognition that
the land I write is not mine, but land stolen from the indigenous people
of Australia (the Nyungar people – the Ballardong – in and around York,
Western Australia). I've known it since being a small child visiting my
uncle's farm, I've known it going to school in the city, going to school in
a country town (Geraldton), and living in the country for a great deal of
my adult life. I've known it living for nearly a decade outside Australia, in
the country and semi-rural places of Cambridgeshire, England and Ohio.
It gnaws at me, it speaks through the poison of loss that inhabits any
landscape where an exploitation of the land has been inextricable from
dispossession. The claim of family being 'early settlers' becomes
inadequate and even horrifying in the face of 80,000 or more years of
Aboriginal habitation and custodianship of the land. Since the 1840s
when my father's family arrived in the south-west of Western Australia,
and began farming there, the bulk of the land has been devastated by
European farming practices, logging (my family were and have been
foresters – from Ireland – as well) mining and a reactive attempt to master
'harsh living conditions.' Survival and damage are tragically linked.

In 1995 a book I'd been slowly working on since the early 1980s was
published in Australia – *The Silo: A Pastoral Symphony*. Though declared

relatively quietly, these issues rose to the surface in my writing it: they were the reasons for its existence. Against the backdrop of Beethoven's Sixth Symphony (the 'Pastoral' Symphony), the paradoxes of beauty and observation and a broader Western aesthetic, and the need to *tell*, were formulated into a very different issue of witness. A darker book followed in 1998 – *The Hunt*. Originally called the *Book of Rural Disasters* and divided into a four-part symphony, it became one relentless undivided sonic unit in terms of construction, and hopefully polyphonic in the voices that emerged from this. I envisaged it as the follow-up to *The Silo*. (In 2000, *The Hierarchy of Sheep* appeared, a hybrid book that pursued the pastoral investigation, with digressions in interest and theme, but it was not a conclusion to a trilogy – it was a cross-roads). And then I imagined a rounding-off to the trilogy with *The New Arcadia*, loosely influenced by, and replying to textualities and tones of, Philip Sidney's brilliant 'old' *Arcadia*. My volume *Peripheral Light: New and Selected Poems* contained a broad selection of new, separate 'rural' poems that were pivotal in my concurrent thinking and work on *The New Arcadia*'s polyphonic poems and book-poem in its entirety.

In writing *The New Arcadia*, I have come to realise that no closure to this pastoral 'life-project' is possible, that the larger pastoral project is connected by subliminal and subtextual threads. I would hope that all my 'pastoral' poetry will eventually form one volume as an active record of observation and interaction. It is a single work around which all my other work revolves. If I am living in or staying in the city (in my childhood the corner block was bush, and a few blocks down the road towards the river was a vast amount of bushland; a little further down was Bateman's farm, so that, even within the city, was the rural), I think about the Western Australian wheatbelt. As a child in a Perth suburb, I spent the days waiting to get back up to the farm outside York, the oldest inland town in Western Australia. At high school I regularly rode my bike out past the town limits of Geraldton (a larger, coastal, rural town) into the scrub and paddocks; at university down in the city I escaped by working on the wheatbins (places of hyper-violence and macho excess) during my holidays, and ploughed on 'Wheatlands,' my uncle's farm which has been the core of my voice. I wandered the bush as a child quoting Keats – the disjunction probably serving me better than quoting any work praising dispossession and clearing!

A surreal sense of being physically welded to the farm, to the wheatbelt, came when I was struck by lightning as fire raged on the world's curve through summer stubble. Then there was a dejected cloud of dependency for years on a farm called 'Happy Valley,' waiting for my shearer-brother to get home and bring conversation from the shearing shed. My strongest bond is to my mother's home at the base of the 'hill that cries,' Walwalinj (Mount Bakewell), the mountain of the central wheatbelt at York, a sacred place of loss and rebirth. It's the place where parrots flock and where deeply painful memories of the many birds and animals I shot in my childhood and youth become almost searing. Memory can be vicious.

I've been literally writing York since my first 'Uncle Jack and the Sheep' poem, drafted when I was thirteen (Uncle Jack didn't trust hobby or weekend farmers who neglected their sheep, not watering them and letting them get fly-blown – though he could spend a moment each afternoon shooting the cockatoos off his giant aerial in order to get better reception on his shaky TV screen). It *is* a 'life project' that has different paddocks and fields, different lenses zooming in or out. It is macro and micro and wide-angle, it's snapshot and time-lapse. Sometimes the same piece of dirt is re-examined at different times of year, and the most fixed character changes as the year changes (and the destruction of the atmosphere and physical earth alters the seasons themselves). Scepticism and drop-jaw wonder are mixed.

The New Arcadia may be an end to the trilogy I mentioned, but it is surrounded by other rural work that concentrates on about 20 square miles of wheatbelt Western Australia, with vistas stretching out through the other places I have lived in. I write it *in situ*, I write it in Cambridge, and I write it in Ohio. It's remarkable how similar and different things are in rural Ohio: corn and soy, as opposed to wheat and now canola 'back home.' Conservative attitudes, 'the church,' xenophobia. The list is endless – through the looking-glass we find ourselves. Consciousness of nation, however, is remarkably different. Australians think isolation in a different way. But that's another story. I write intensely about a single region from an often international perspective and geography, but it's no less of that specific place for all this. It's a matter of differing angles.

An anarchist vegan pacifist, my attitudes to the exploitation of people, animals, and land will not be entirely the same as those of my family and friends, but that makes me no less close to them. I don't believe in nations or countries, but I do believe in communities, even when our individual beliefs are so different. I believe in us having a direct say in how we live our lives, and not in others purporting to represent our views. I believe that the natural environment should be protected at all cost. But I know something about growing food – which I have done on a small and a large scale, and I know how much hay itches during hay carting. I also love Dante and Baudelaire and Rimbaud and Whitman and the list is endless: all different co-ordinates on a language tree at times violent and self-serving, at others linguistically liberating. I believe in peaceful rebellion but not revolution: change comes by example and observation and respect.

The New Arcadia respects its sources, but is its own anti-epic lyrical poem. Many small parts making a whole – almost a discontinuous narrative, it's the story without the explanation. The roads – the journeys – are there, but when and how we take them is up to how we read individually. I hope none of these poems are mere photographs: it's not just a book of memory, though variety and variegations of memory are pivotal, but a living work. I don't want to capture the sound and colours of the bird before it becomes extinct, but help gain recognition for its beauty and necessity and stop the clearing of its habitat, the urge for profit, the indifference. We need to eat, we need 'space,' we need our sense of achievement, but not at the expense of all else and all other living things. Space is infinite in a square foot of earth, and by looking close to hand, and inwards, vast horizons present themselves.

While the title of the book carries its ironies – there never has been and increasingly never can be an arcadia in a world drowned in pesticide, herbicide, corporate farms, animal abuse and indifference to indigenous claims to the land, there *can* be arcadias at our feet, at our fingertips. So, start with what we have: the micro can become the macro, then who knows? For me, it's never too late. Poetry for me is activism.

David Butler

WHO WAS ALEXANDRE O'NEILL AND WHY SHOULD WE
READ HIM ?

Alexandre Manuel Vahia de Castro O'Neill (1924-1986) is a major
Portuguese poet of Irish descent, related to the O'Neills of Clanboy. He
chose O'Neill, the surname of his maternal grandmother, as pen-name,
and once joked to his friend Fernando Correia da Silva, 'I am the son of
an Irish lord. I will take possession of those emerald estates when my
father kicks the bucket. This waiting makes me impatient, since I am
very fond of Irish coffee and of the shamrock. . .'
    For most of his life the politics of Portugal were dominated by the
dictatorship of António Salazar, who came to power in 1932, and whose
regime wasn't finally overthrown until the bloodless 'Carnation Revolution'
of 1974. O'Neill remained an acute critic of the regime, lambasting in his
poetry the climate of fear and inaction that its repressive policies brought
about. He was also a critic of Western adventures such as the American
imbroglio in Vietnam, and in *Saldos no Vietname* wrote presciently of the
collateral damage wrought by high technology bombs, which fall *'onde o
americano espera nunca estar'* ('where no American expects ever to be').
But what makes O'Neill of particular interest is the irony, humour and
erotic play that underlies his work. These are of course stubbornly
personal qualities, and their celebration within a politically repressive
environment always carries a subversive edge.
    O'Neill was quite a romantic figure, and in 1949 had fallen in love
with Nora Mitrani, a French surrealist who was in Lisbon at the time.
But several years later he was refused a passport by the security police
(*Polícia Internacional de Defesa do Estado*, or PIDE), and so could not follow
her to Paris. Although O'Neill was twice married and twice divorced,
Mitrani remained the great love of his life, and her suicide in 1961 led to
some of his darkest and most intense work. In particular, in 1962 he
wrote an extended meditation on her suicide, while, some years earlier,
the forced separation from her led to the composition of *Um Adeus
Português*, considered by many to be one of the great Portuguese poems
of the century.
    But there are other, lighter strains to O'Neill's poetry. He was greatly
influenced both by the French Symbolists and the Surrealists, and at
twenty-four was one of the founders of *Movimento Surrealista de Lisboa*,
Lisbon's Surrealist Movement, though he broke with this movement
several years later. He also worked very successfully in advertising, and
much of his poetry delights in pun, in wordplay and in the physical

appearance of the word on the page. Thus, in a line such as 'um conde que cora ao ser condecorado', literally 'a Count who blushes when decorated', the participle 'condecorado' is composed of 'conde' ('count') and 'corado' ('blushing'). This also makes O'Neill particularly difficult to translate, and it would be a great disservice not to present the following selection from his work in a bilingual format.

AUTO-RETRATO

O'Neill (Alexandre), moreno português,
cabelo asa de corvo; da angústia da cara,
nariguete que sobrepunha de través
a ferida desdenhosa e não cicatrizada.
Se a visagem de tal sujeito é o que vês
(omita-se o olho triste e a testa iluminada)
o retrato moral também tem os seus quês
(aqui, uma pequena frase censurada. . .)
 No amor? No amor crê (ou não fosse ele O'Neill!)
 e tem a veleidade de o saber fazer
 (pois amor não há feito) das maneiras mil
que são a semovente estátua do prazer.
Mas sofre de ternura, bebe de mais e ri-se
do que neste soneto sobre si mesmo disse. . .

SELF-PORTRAIT

O'Neill (Alexandre), a swarthy Portuguese,
hair a crow's wing; of anxious face,
a thin nose set cross-ways above
the disdainful wound that hasn't scarred over.
If it's the face of this subject that you see
(let's forget the sad eye and illumined brow)
the moral portrait also has its qualities
(here, a short phrase has been censured...)
Regarding love? He believes in love (or he wouldn't be an O'Neill!)
and has the whim to know how to make it
(since love doesn't come ready-made) in the thousand manners
which go to make up the self-moving statue of pleasure.
But he suffers tenderness, drinks too much, and laughs
at that which in this sonnet he says about himself...

SONETOS GARANTIDOS

Sonetos garantidos por dois anos.
E é muito já, leitor que mos compraste
Para encontrar a alma, que trocaste
Por rádios, frigoríficos, enganos. . .
Essa tristeza sobre pernas faz-te
Temeroso e cruel e tonto e traste.
Nem pior nem melhor que outros fulanos,
Não vês a Bomba e crês nos marcianos. . .
E é para ti que escrevo, é para ti
Que um verso lanço – ó mão! – como o destino,
e nele ponho mesura, desatino,
Rasgo, invenção, lugar-comum, protesto?
Antes para soldado ou para resto,
Escroto de velho, ronco de suíno. . .

SONNETS GUARANTEED

Sonnets guaranteed for two years.
And it's already a lot, reader who bought them from me
To find a soul, which you've bartered
For radios, fridges, deceptions…
That sadness on legs makes you
Fearful and cruel and stupid and worthless,
Neither better nor worse than the other wasters,
You don't see the Bomb and you believe in Martians…
And is it for you that I write, is it for you
That I hurl my verse – o hand! – like destiny,
And in it place courtesy, folly,
Rupture, invention, cliché, protest?
Sooner for the soldier, or the riff-raff,
Old man's scrotum, hog's snore…

UM ADEUS PORTUGUÊS

Nos teus olhos altamente perigosos
vigora ainda o mais rigoroso amor
a luz dos ombros pura e a sombra
duma angústia já purificada

Não tu não podias ficar presa comigo
à roda em que apodreço
apodrecemos
a esta pata ensanguentada que vacila
quase medita
e avança mugindo pelo túnel
de uma velha dor

Não podias ficar nesta cadeira
onde passo o dia burocrático
o dia-a-dia da miséria
que sobe aos olhos vem às mãos
aos sorrisos
ao amor mal soletrado
à estupidez ao desespero sem boca
ao medo perfilado
à alegria sonâmbula à vírgula maníaca
do modo funcionário de viver

Não podias ficar nesta cama comigo
em trânsito mortal até ao dia sórdido
canino
policial
até ao dia que não vem da promessa
puríssima da madrugada
mas da miséria de uma noite gerada
por um dia igual

Não podias ficar presa comigo
à pequena dor que cada um de nós
traz docemente pela mão
a esta pequena dor à portuguesa
tão mansa quase vegetal

Mas tu não mereces esta cidade não mereces
esta roda de náusea em que giramos
até à idiotia
esta pequena morte
e o seu minucioso e porco ritual
esta nossa razão absurda de ser

Não tu és da cidade aventureira
da cidade onde o amor encontra as suas ruas
e o cemitério ardente
da sua morte
tu és da cidade onde vives por um fio
de puro acaso
onde morres ou vives não de asfixia
mas às mãos de uma aventura de um comércio puro
sem a moeda falsa do bem e do mal

Nesta curva tão terna e lancinante
que vai ser que já é o teu desaparecimento
digo-te adeus
e como um adolescente
tropeço de ternura
por ti.

A PORTUGUESE FAREWELL

In your highly dangerous eyes
there still reigns the most rigorous love
the pure light from shoulders and the shadow
of an anxiety that is already purified

No, you could not remain a prisoner with me
of the wheel in which I rot away
we rot away
of this bloody paw that hesitates
almost meditates
and than advances lowing through the tunnel
of an old pain

You could not remain in this chair
where I pass the bureaucratic day
the day-in-day-out of misery
which rises to the eyes enters into the hands
into the smiles
into the badly spelt-out love
into the stupidity the mouthless despair
into the regimented fear
the sleepwalking joy the manic punctuation
of the functionary's way of life

You could not stay in this bed with me
in mortal transit towards the sordid day
the dog-day
the police day
towards that day which does not come out of
the most pure promise of the dawn
but from the misery of a night begotten
of an identical day

You could not remain a prisoner with me
of the tiny pain that every one of us
carries gently by the hand
that tiny pain *à la portuguèse*
that is so tame it is almost vegetal

No you did not deserve this city did not deserve
this wheel of nausea in which we run around
until brain dead
this petty death
with its painstaking and filthy ritual
this, our absurd *raison d'être*

No you are from that adventurous city
from the city where love encounters her streets
and the burning cemetery
of her death
you are from the city where life hangs by a thread
of pure chance
where you die or you live not from asphyxia
but at the hands of a venture of pure commerce
without the false coin of good and evil

At this bend, so tender and thrusting
which your absence will be and already is
I bid you farewell
and like an adolescent
I trip up with tenderness
for you.

– translations by **David Butler**

Elizabeth Mac Donald

MARIO LUZI

It is an unseasonably cold afternoon in Florence. From the fifth floor of
an apartment block off the Arno quays, I look out on the city skyline in
the gathering dusk. Mario Luzi invites me to take a seat opposite him in
his study, where every available space is crammed with books, and
unhung paintings are stacked in a corner.

I ask him how he is. He folds his hands quietly in his lap. 'I haven't
been feeling very well recently,' he says, and shakes his head. He looks
out at me from brown eyes that have been dimmed with age, and I catch
the melancholy there. Impetuously, I rush in to assure him that he is
indeed looking well. He shakes his head again and says nothing. I fill the
silence by recalling the celebrations in Florence for his ninetieth birthday
back on 20 October 2004, when he was made a life senator. This honour,
along with many others including an honorary doctorate from Queen's,
sit with disarming lightness on his shoulders. He smiles gently.

Mario Luzi's career as a poet spanned seven decades and twice earned
him a nomination for the Nobel Prize for literature. His first collection
(*La barca*) appeared in 1935 when he was twenty-one years of age. Despite
his youth, his talent was immediately recognised, and in particular his
'exemplary imagination' (Carlo Bo). With this collection he established
himself as a member of the 'hermetic' movement. Founded in the 1920s
by Giuseppe Ungaretti and Eugenio Montale, by 1940 Luzi had become
one of its leading exponents with collections such as *Avvento notturno*
(1940), *Un brindisi* (1946) and *Quaderno gotico* (1947). His poetry at this
time is characterized by an affinity with Symbolism, resulting in allusive
lyrics of great beauty and remarkable technical mastery.

Nevertheless, even at this early stage, certain enduring themes are
evident. Luzi was a young man during World War II, and this gave rise to
his preoccupation with the effects of war and violence, and the absence
of liberty. His poetry can be seen as a tireless exploration of the negative
effects of history. Another recurring motif also present is Luzi's certainty
of the spiritual nature of the universe. For him, this offered a means for
intuitive understanding complementary to the lessons of history.

From the 1950s onwards then, the Hermetic phase was not abandoned,
but rather amplified and enlarged upon, producing collections such as
Primizie del deserto (1952), *Onore del vero* (1957), *Il giusto della vita* (1960).
Then in 1963 came a turning point. With the collection *Nel magma* came a
need to delve into contingency, giving rise to a style less reliant on
aesthetic perfection and more prose-orientated. This afforded Luzi scope

for grappling with juxtaposed themes such as time and eternity, change and identity, being and becoming. Such is the sway that time holds over our lives, he remarked, that man can conceive of eternity only as an infinite quantity of time. To this period belong other collections such as *Dal fondo delle campagne* (1965), *Su fondamenti invisibili* (1971), *Al fuoco della controversia* (1978), *Per il battesimo dei nostri frammenti* (1985), *Frasi e incisi di un canto salutare* (1990).

The last great period opens with *Viaggio terrestre e celeste di Simone Martini* (1994), and concludes with *Dottrina dell' estremo principiante* (2004). This late flowering has produced poetry of a crystalline beauty, permeated by an exploration of the transcendental. Never a mere magnifying glass, Luzi's poetry here acquires the qualities of a prism, in which the play of light and colour throw into relief a mind questing for meaning and truth.

Mario Luzi had ties of affection with Ireland, and visited the country on a few occasions. He was intrigued by a certain mystery inherent in the country, occasioned by the contrast between a genial surface, under which something darker could sometimes be glimpsed. Never a fan of Mussolini's, who knows but that his fondness for the country didn't begin with the firearm attack he recalled being carried out against *Il Duce* by an Irish tourist.

Luzi was an outspoken critic of the present centre-right government in Italy, comparing Italian Prime Minister Silvio Berlusconi to a modern-day Samson, tearing down the institutions of the country and trampling under foot the constitution. Evidently, when Berlusconi rang to congratulate him on his elevation to life senator, he commenced the phone call by reminding Luzi that he was his editor. This is indeed true: Luzi's publishing house is part of the giant conglomerate Mondadori owned by Silvio Berlusconi.

Mario Luzi belongs to an artistic elect, representing, perhaps, a new frontier of alternativism. He is one of the very few great artists in whom the polarizing divisions of Yeat's dictum, that there can be perfection of either the life or the work, have been healed. His lasting testimony is to show how, instead, life and work can feed seamlessly and creatively into each other.

Just four days after our interview, Mario Luzi died peacefully in his sleep on Monday, 28 February 2005. Ar dheis Dé go raibh a anam.

Elizabeth Mac Donald's interview with Mario Luzi will be published in *Poetry Ireland Review* 83.

Mario Luzi, 1914-2005

ALLA VITA

Amici ci aspetta una barca e dondola
nella luce ove il cielo s'inarca
e tocca il mare,
volano creature pazze ad amare
il viso d'Iddio caldo di speranza
in alto in basso cercando
affetto in ogni occulta distanza
e piangono: noi siamo in terra
ma ci potremo un giorno librare
esilmente piegare sul seno divino
come rose dai muri nelle strade odorose
sul bimbo che le chiede senza voce.

Amici dalla barca si vede il mondo
e in lui una verità che procede
intrepida, un sospiro profondo
dalle foci alle sorgenti;
la Madonna dagli occhi trasparenti
scende adagio incontro ai morenti,
raccoglie il cumulo della vita, i dolori
le voglie segrete da anni sulla faccia inumidita.
Le ragazze alla finestra annerita
con lo sguardo verso i monti
non sanno finire d'aspettare l'avvenire.

Nelle stanze la voce materna
senza origine, senza profondità s'alterna
col silenzio della terra, è bella
e tutto par nato da quella.

– da *La barca* (1935)

Mario Luzi

TO LIFE

My friends, a boat awaits us rocking in the light
where the sky curves down
and touches the sea,
and creatures fly in a frenzy of love for
the hope-radiant face of God
high up and low down they seek
affection in every occult distance
and cry: We are on this earth
but one day shall float free
and delicately settle on the divine breast
like roses from the walls along scented roads
on the child who asks for them wordlessly.

My friends, from the boat you can see the world
and in it a truth that advances
intrepidly, a deep sigh running
from river mouth to source;
with lucent eyes Our Lady
glides slowly down towards the dying,
and gathers to her a lifetime's pile of grief
and secret desires etched years ago on tear-stained faces.
The young girls at a darkened window
their eyes turned to the mountains
are never done with waiting for the future.

Within the rooms the maternal voice is a wellspring
beginningless, bottomless, alternating
with the silence of the earth, a beauty
from which everything seems to have been born.

– translated by **Elizabeth Mac Donald**

Gerald Dawe

JOHN BERRYMAN: FATAL ATTRACTIONS

> 'Literature in my early days was still something you lived by; you
> absorbed it, you took it into your system. Not as a connoisseur, aesthete,
> lover of literature. No, it was something on which you formed your life,
> which you ingested, so that it became part of your substance, your path
> to liberation and full freedom. All that began to disappear, was already
> disappearing, when I was young.' – Saul Bellow, *It All Adds Up* (323-24).

I

In his memoir about John Berryman's stay in Dublin in 1966-67, John
Montague describes the man he met in the Majestic Hotel, Baggot
Street, as 'enthusiastic, hilarious, drunken, as splendid and generous a
man as one might meet, who fitted into the roar of Dublin pub life with
ease' (Montague: 202). Some twelve years earlier, Montague had met a
completely different Berryman in Iowa: 'nervous, taut, arrogant, uneasy;
very nearly a caricature of the over-trained, fiercely cerebral, academic
poet of the Fifties; a man hair-triggered for insult, and quite capable of
getting angry with a student' (Montague: 202). Which is precisely what
happened 'one autumn evening in that second week of term; Berryman
hit or at least scuffled with someone and was landed in jail.' He was
dismissed subsequently from his post.

The previous November (1953), Berryman had witnessed the final
days of Dylan Thomas's life, Thomas having collapsed into a coma in the
Chelsea Hotel where both poets were staying. They had previously met
quite some time back, in March 1937 in England, when the twenty-three
year old Berryman was a graduate student at Cambridge and Thomas
had come to St John's College to give a reading. Thomas went on a binge
for the week he stayed there and Berryman followed suit, only to enter,
in the words of his biographer, John Haffenden, 'a period of despondency
lasting at least another week, worrying his sense of incompetence and
unfilled ambition' (Haffenden: 89). The next month Berryman made his
first trip to Ireland only to discover that the object of his journey, W B
Yeats, was in London. (Curious to think that had Berryman left the trip
until August 1937 his path may have crossed with Antonin Artaud who
began his crazed stay in Ireland then). Undeterred, Berryman wrote to
Yeats and a meeting was arranged for Friday 16 April at the Athenaeum
Club in London.

As Berryman recounts in his *Paris Review* interview (1971), Thomas
shows up again:

Thomas had very nearly succeeded in getting me drunk earlier in the
day. He was full of scorn for Yeats, as he was for Eliot, Pound, Auden.
He thought my admiration for Yeats was the funniest thing in that part
of London. It wasn't until about three o'clock that I realised that he and
I were drinking more than usual. I didn't drink much at that time;
Thomas drank much more than I did. I had the sense to leave [and] just
made it for the appointment. (Plimpton: 304)

From the wide eyed grad-student poet of the Thirties to the thrice-
married, world-weary poet teacher of the Sixties, Berryman's relatively
short life (he died at the age of 58) reveals a fatal attraction to self-
destruction perversely echoed throughout his generation of American
writers and painters, whose constant companions seemed to be alcoholism
and depression. As Robert Lowell has it in one of his valedictory poems,
'For John Berryman':

> Yet really we had the same life
> the generic one
> our generation offered.   (*Collected Poems*: 737)

In the Afterword to her memoir, *Poets in their Youth*, Eileen Simpson lists
the fallen: Dylan Thomas, Theodore Roethke, Randall Jarrell, Richard
(R P) Blackmur, Delmore Schwartz, and, by extension, Louis MacNeice
(one-time drinking buddy of both Berryman and Thomas) and Robert
Lowell, who outlived Berryman. All had died at (relatively speaking) an
early age (Simpson: 239). The transformation which Montague noted in
his memoir is, nevertheless, shocking, and all the more so when one
bears in mind Montague's own gloss on Berryman's writing life:

> This is something I want to make clear: Berryman is the only writer I
> have ever seen for whom drink seemed to be a positive stimulus. He
> drank enormously and smoked heavily, but it seemed to be part of a
> pattern of work, a crashing of the brain barriers as he raced towards the
> completion of the *Dream Songs*... He had come into his own and radiat-
> ed the psychic electricity of genius (Montague: 202).

In John Montague's view, Berryman thrived in that 'glorious year,' living
in a 'trim suburban villa' in Ballsbridge, a regular of Ryan's Bar. Indeed,
Montague recalls taking Berryman to meet Garech Browne, and at a
party in the Dublin hills, 'John seemed to be drinking at random':

> There was a tray on the lawn, for instance, and instead of keeping to one
> drink [Berryman] just poured whatever was nearest to him into his glass,
> whisky, gin, vodka, white wine, an impossible mixture (Montague: 205).

Anyone who has seen that kind of manic drinking knows how lethal it becomes for the alcoholic. Again Montague's memoir takes up the story not long before Berryman took his own life. At a reading he gives at the University of Minnesota, Montague meets Berryman again, on this occasion a relic of his former self:

> He shuffled out of an Alcoholics Anonymous lecture, hands twitching, face pale and uneasy as he greeted me...The contrast between our previous meetings in Dublin when he would roar out his latest dream songs, good, bad, or indifferent, lovely or awful or 'delicious' (his own phrase for praise), was too abrupt. (Montague: 206).

Berryman seemed 'clearly ill at ease in such a restrained life' and, according to Montague, the reason was clear. '[N] ot only his habits but his habits of work were linked with drink; the ramshackle structure of the *Dream Songs* is based as much upon the ups and downs of the chronic drunk as anything else.' This transformation towards the close of his life, and the all too short respite of his final year with the birth of his second daughter – 'eleven months of abstinence, half a year of prolific rebirth, then suicide,' as Lowell defined it (Hamilton: 440) – is mirrored in the earlier shift of self-image.

From that 'academic poet of the Fifties' described by Saul Bellow as 'The Princeton John' – 'tallish, slender, nervous' who had 'many signs that he was inhibiting erratic impulses' (Bellow: 267), into the long bearded, guru-like Beat figure of the late Sixties, 'High shouldered in his thin coat and big homburg, bearded, [who] coughed up phlegm [and] looked decayed' (Bellow: 271), Berryman ends up a haunted version of himself. The changes might have been liberating for the hidebound Berryman even while producing the claustrophobic hothouse atmosphere of many of the *Dream Songs*. At another level they were to prove distorting and costly. Could it really be this 'easy' to make up poems for Henry to think and say? The constant need for the reaffirmation of his friends' approval seems to suggest otherwise. The scholarly side of Berryman's training probably cast some inner doubt, but by that stage the bardic persona had won and there was no way out. The mask had stuck.

Berryman, the elegist of his generation of fellow poet-teachers who burned out on ambition, alcohol, drugs and depression, is a talismanic figure, representative of a literary culture that in the decade following his death also passed away. As the headily politicised Seventies and Eighties scorned the apparent egotism and introversion of the 'victim-hero' poets, by the Nineties poetry was viewed much more as a career than as a complex fate.

So perhaps the tangled lives of Berryman's generation have in fact more in common with today's 'pop' culture than would have seemed possible 10 or 15 years ago. The culture that Berryman and his generation embraced, almost in spite of its antipathetic nature, is told with great verve by one of Berryman's good friends, Saul Bellow, in *Herzog* (1964) and in *Humboldt's Gift* (1975). Based on Delmore Schwartz, the character of Von Humboldt Fleisher is emblematic of the angst and ambition of that fateful generation. Here narrator Charlie Citrine meditates on the significance of Humboldt's death:

> For after all Humboldt did what poets in crass America are supposed to do. He chased ruin and death even harder than he chased women. He blew his talent and his health and reached home, the grave in a dusty slide. He plowed himself under. Okay. So did Edgar Allen Poe, picked out of a Baltimore gutter. And Hart Crane over the side of a ship. And Jarrell falling in front of a car. And poor John Berryman jumping from a bridge. For some reason this awfulness is peculiarly appreciated by business and technological America. The country is proud of its dead poets. It takes terrific satisfaction in the poets' testimony that the USA is too tough, too big, too much, too rugged, that American reality is overpowering. And to be a poet is a school thing, a skirt thing, a church thing. (Bellow: 118)

Echoing Montague's view, Saul Bellow recalls in 1973 the real-life Berryman in the following stark terms: 'Inspiration contained a death threat. He would, as he wrote the things he had waited and prayed for, fall apart. Drink was a stabilizer. It somewhat reduced the fatal intensity' (Bellow: 270).

II

Berryman's writing life prefigures many of the features of contemporary 'lifestyle' popular culture. From the iconic Chelsea Hotel* where Berryman held vigil over Dylan Thomas's last days (and Thomas was of course to become immortalised as one of the great folk heroes of the Sixties), to his own death almost twenty years later in January 1971, Berryman's life story is so familiar today. Even the manner of his death has the ring of rock myth about it. He 'walked unto the west end of the Washington Avenue Bridge high over the Mississippi River' and 'at about nine o'clock,' according to one eye-witness, 'jumped up on the railing, sat down and quickly leaned forward [and] never looked back.' The *Minneapolis Star*, Haffenden recounts, 'reported a witness who observed that he apparently "waved goodbye"' (Haffenden: 419).

The rock hero beset by the search for calibrated pre-eminence and celebrity, shifting from gig to gig (albeit with universities as the venues), the late night speak-*fest*, ceaseless drinking, ultimate addiction, the non-stop touring and the temporary respite – all have the hallmarks of a 'star' on the move and (alas) on the wane. What Berryman felt he was losing back home in the pressure cooker literary world of America, he tried to restore in the intimate yet oddly respectful space of his brief life in Dublin. Some of the best of the *Dream Songs* is the result.

'Ireland' provided a source of fascination and inspiration for Berryman in the shape of the 'majestic shade' of Yeats, and latterly there was the fatal allure of the infamous 'drink' culture (like a moth to the flame). With booze so much a part of the literary culture, who would notice another literary genius in the corner? He could fit in, at last. His looks were even part of the fashion of the time. Indeed it is curious to compare Berryman's generation with the parallel Irish generation of the Forties and Fifties as they struggled with addiction and depression – Flann O'Brien, Brendan Behan, Patrick Kavanagh, among others. It is also interesting to note in conclusion that fellow American poet-teacher, the much-troubled Theodore Roethke ('a daring & true & beautiful poet' in Berryman's words, Haffenden: 331), had been there before Berryman when he visited (and had been hospitalised) in the country in 1960. But therein lies another story of loss and obsession.

Note

*Home to numerous mythological rock heroes such as Janis Joplin, who also died well before her time – Leonard Cohen's elegy on Joplin, 'The Chelsea Hotel' might serve as a moving coda to Berryman's own tragedy, with the necessary gender-change, of course:

> I remember you well in the Chelsea Hotel,
> you were famous, your heart was a legend.
> You told me again you preferred handsome men,
> but for me you would make an exception.
> And clenching your fist for the ones like us
> who are oppressed by the figures of beauty,
> you fixed yourself, you said, 'Well, never mind,
> we are ugly, but we have the music.'   (Cohen: 197)

References

Saul Bellow, *Humboldt's Gift* (London, 1975)
Saul Bellow, *It All Adds Up* (London, 1994)
Leonard Cohen, *Stranger Music: Selected Poems and Songs* (London, 1993)
John Haffenden, *The life of John Berryman* (London, 1982)
Ian Hamilton, *Robert Lowell: A Biography* (London, 1983)
Robert Lowell, *Collected Poems* (London, 2003)
John Montague, *The figure in the Cave and other essays* (Dublin, 1989)
George Plimpton (Ed), *The Paris Review Interviews: Writers at Work*, 4th Series (London, 1982)
Eileen Simpson, *Poets in their Youth* (London, 1982)

Mary O'Donnell

REFLECTIONS ON INGEBORG BACHMANN

Ingeborg Bachmann once wrote that love triumphs, and death too, because death's triumph is time itself. When her own death came, it was through fire. Based then in Rome and absorbed by work on a prose trilogy (one novel of which, *Malina*, was published during her life), she took some tranquillisers on the night of 26 September 1973, determined to sleep. She got into bed and lit a cigarette. When she awoke, her night-clothes were on fire. She stumbled to the shower and managed to extinguish the flames, then ran the bathwater to further cool the burns. Only then did she phone a friend. The doctors at the Sant' Eugenio clinic could not save her. Forty percent of her skin had been burned and the writer died on 17 October 1973.

Ingeborg Bachmann was one of the few German women writers, apart from Christa Wolf, who became established as an important European writer in the latter half of the twentieth century. Born in the Austrian town of Klagenfurt in 1926, the daughter of a grammar-school teacher, she studied philosophy, psychology and Germanistics at Innsbruck, Graz and Vienna, and in 1950 completed a doctoral thesis on Heidegger; but poetry, not philosophy, became the genre for which she was eventually celebrated. By 1953 she was one of the talented younger women who graced the largely masculine scene of the Gruppe 47 writers' association, winning in that year the influential Gruppe 47 poetry prize. Between then and her death in 1973, she received many more awards for her work, including the Bremen Literature Prize and the Georg-Büchner-Prize.

Apart from poetry, Bachmann wrote radio plays dating back to the time when she worked for the Viennese radio station Rot/Weiss/Rot. Her prose, including many fragments, consists of an inexhaustible range of variations on established themes. When awarded the Hörspielpreis der Kriegsblinden in 1959, Bachmann referred publicly to hidden pain as an inherent aspect of human nature which, when recognised, activates our instinct to advance towards perfection in every sphere of experience. It is this world of values about which – unlike Wittgenstein's view in the *Tractatus* – the writer is free to articulate, and to which Ingeborg Bachmann attuned her artistic and aesthetic energies throughout her short life.

Influenced by Wittgenstein and Musil, as well as the post-war poet Paul Celan (whom she first met in Vienna at the end of 1947), she displayed a critical attitude to language and tradition, with major themes in her poetry springing from her experience of the occupation of Austria in 1938 when she was twelve years old, the horrors of the war and the

Holocaust itself. Beyond this, and deriving from it, lay her sense that history was always doomed to self-replicate. The warning 'Es kommen härtere Tage' from the title poem of the collection *Die gestundete Zeit* (*Time-lapse*) demonstrates this intensity of feeling, although the poem is both spare and restrained. She implies rather than exhorts, as in 'Holz und Späne' ('Wood and Splinters'). The title poem of her second collection, *Anrufung des Großen Bären* (*Invoking the Great Bear*) denounces the misuse of power inherent in any organised ideology. Apart from the biblical and mythological connotations of the sign of the Great Bear, it was also used by Simone Weil (as 'das Grosse Tier') and Bachmann draws attention to this link in her 1955 essay on the philosopher.

By no means an 'easy' writer, the task of translating a selection of Ingeborg Bachmann's work began for me as far back as 1987, when I worked on some poems from *Anrufung des Großen Bären*. I felt automatically attracted to Bachmann's abstractions, to the fact that for her the concrete 'telling detail' – nowadays so unquestioned – seemed not always to represent an essential characteristic of poetry. There is a melancholy and, sometimes in opposition to this, an elevated, heightened tone which works within the poetry and makes it a challenging proposition, not least of all because thematically she offers no obvious formulae, no codes for survival during our transient encounter with self and others in the world.

Ingeborg Bachmann was a Bohemian. Despite a solidly bourgeois belief in the totality of the individual and individual concerns, her life-long allegiance was to the value of two things – art and love. She was intolerant of anything less than perfection, the ideal, the absolute commitment, and her late poem 'Bohmen liegt am Meer'/ 'Bohemia is by the Sea' shows her to be '...a Bohemian, gypsy, owning nothing, keeping nothing, / still negotiating the cantankerous sea, to catch sight / of the land of my choosing.'

I have not included her juvenilia in the following selection. I suspect that Bachmann herself might not care for it very much in hindsight, although of course I cannot know this. The kernel of her work appears from 1948 onwards, when she finally sheds the excesses of the tragic-romantic posturing which characterised the earliest material and began a committed exploration of the formal and structural aspects of poetry, gradually asserting an unstinting control even within the free verse work found side-by-side with regular rhymed stanzas. She was both a superb technician as well as philosopher: living within a society which was not, by and large in those post-war years anti-intellectual, this was not seen to be detrimental. If anything, her highly calibrated intellectual sweep informs the poetry and contributes to its challenge.

During her life, Bachmann's interest in music resulted in collaborations on a number of projects with the composer Hans Werner

Henze, who was a close friend. By the end of the 1950s, when she had written libretti for a ballet and an opera by Henze, as well as having produced a number of radio plays (with music by Henze), her work had undergone a critical transformation, and the nature of this reappraisal was reflected in her lectures at Frankfurt University.

Die gestundete Zeit fairly vibrates with absences, despite the often inhabited, even cluttered settings of some of the poems. Whether she is in England, Paris, or Munich, Bachmann never loses sight of the possibility of 'harder times' ahead. The good is on loan, as it were, time has lapsed and very likely will recover from its comfortable, if transient, loss of form. She draws succour from the natural cycles, from seed spread ('Sterne im März' / 'Stars in March'), from the sight of rivers, rain and light, recognising all the time that history may have 'booked us a grave, / from which there is no resurrection.'

At times, Bachmann creates apocalyptic scenarios, as in the poem 'Vision', which announces

> When these ships come ashore…
> We shall die like the net-hauled fish,
> that rock around them on the widening swell
> to thousandfold corpses!

Yet she inhabits an almost Kierkegaardian realm, whereby absences within the multiplicities of human experience are recognised, and despite that recognition comes the knowledge that survival can only happen when risk is taken: risk in living, in writing, in loving, in not leaning into the (in its own way) possibly commendable but ultimately corrupting peace of the bourgeois. Bachmann brings us tasty and testy words: salt and bread, a storm of roses, psalms, images of the shore and the land, of fish and knives and waves cut by knives, of skeletons and earthquakes, of thickets and constellations, of treacherous lovers with whom one inhabits a 'fog-land.' All the time, the ceaseless quest for enlightenment, which for Bachmann is experienced through love and art, through the guiding aesthetic principle. Truth, she warns in 'Was wahr ist' ('Truth') is difficult. It does not guarantee the space one imagines. It might – she suggests – ultimately lead towards the unknown exit within one's existential prison. Either way, one is compelled to look in poems which incorporate elements of an imagined exotic 'south' ('Lieder von einer Insel' / 'Songs from an Island') with something much chillier, withdrawn and internalised.

Bachmann stands as witness to many things not literally named, but suggested and anticipated in the apocalyptic visions of fire and deluge, of flight from the enemy and asylum – always temporary – in other restive landscapes.

Ingeborg Bachmann

NIGHT FLIGHT

Our land is the sky,
tilled by the sweat of engines,
in the face of night,
risking dreams –

dreamt from skullspots and pyres,
beneath the roof of the world, whose tiles
were carried off by the wind – and then rain, rain,
rain in our house and in the mills
the blind flights of bats.
Who lived there? Whose hands were pure?
Who lit the night,
haunted the spectres?

Concealed in feathers of steel, instruments,
timers and dials interrogate space,
the cloud-bushes, touch the body
of our hearts' forgotten language:
short long long. . . For an hour
hailstones beat on the ear's drum,
which, turned against us, listens and distorts.

The sun and Earth have not set,
merely wandered like unknown constellations.

We have risen from a harbour
where to return doesn't count
not cargo not booty.
India's spice and silks from Japan
belong to the handlers
as fish to the nets.

Yet there's a smell,
forerunners of comets
and the wind's web,
shredded by fallen comets.
Call it the status of the lonely,
for whom amazement happens.

Nothing further.

We have arisen, and the convents are empty,
since we endure, an order which does not cure
and does not instruct. To bargain is not
the pilots' business. They have
set their sights and spread on their knees
the map of a world, to which nothing is added.

Who lives down there? Who weeps. . .
Who loses the key to the house?
Who can't find his bed, who sleeps
on doorsteps? Who, when morning comes,
dares to point at the silver stripes: look, above me. . .
When the new water grips the millwheel,
who dares to remember the night?

INVOKING THE GREAT BEAR

Great Bear, come down, shaggy night,
cloud-pelted animal with ancient eyes,
starred eyes,
your glistening paws break
through the thicket with claws,
starred claws,
wary we cling to the hearth,
yet entranced by you, we distrust
your weary flanks and the sharp
half-stripped teeth,
ancient Bear.

A fir-cone: your human world.
The cone-scales: you.
I drive it, roll it
from the first forests
to the forests at the end,
snort at it, taste it in my mouth
and seize it with my paws.

Fear or fear not!
Pay to the beggar's pouch and spare

a kind word for the blind man,
that he may hold the bear to the leash.
And season the lamb well.

Could be, that this bear
rips himself loose, no longer menaces,
hunts the cones that fell from the firs,
the great, the winged,
that plunged from Paradise.

STARS IN MARCH

The seed is spread. Fields
rise up in the rain and stars of March.
In the formula of barren ideas
the universe complies with the example
of light, which does not stir the snow.

Beneath the snow there's also dust
and, what doesn't decay, the dust's
later nourishment. O starting wind!
Once more, ploughs rip up the darkness.
The days want to lengthen.

On long days someone seeds us, unasked,
in those straight and crooked lines,
and the stars give out. In the fields,
we thrive or rot, without choice,
docile as rain and also, finally, light.

FOG-LAND

In winter my lover thrives
among the forest creatures.
The laughing fox knows I must return
before morning.
How the clouds tremble! And a layer
of broken ice falls on me
from the snow craters.

In winter my lover
is a tree among trees inviting
the melancholic crows
to its lovely branches. She knows
that at dusk, the wind will raise
her stiff adorned evening gown
and chase me home.

In winter my lover
swims mute among the fish.
On the bank, I stand in thrall to waters,
caressed from within
by the stroke of her fins.
I watch as she dips and turns,
till banished by the floes.

And warned once more by the shriek
of the bird that arcs stiffly
above, I head for the open field: there
she plucks the hens bald,
throws me a white collarbone.
I wield it to my throat,
make my way through the scattered plumage.

A faithless lover, as well I know,
at times she sweeps into town
in her high-heels,
she parades herself in bars, the straw
from her glass deep in her mouth,
the *mot juste* tripping from her lips.
I do not understand this language.

I have seen fog-land,
I have eaten the smoke-screened heart.

– translations by **Mary O'Donnell**

Andrew Fitzsimons

AN INTERVIEW WITH THOMAS KINSELLA

This interview took place in Dublin on Tuesday, 17 August 2004, and
began with a discussion of Kinsella's current project, *Readings in Poetry*, a
Peppercanister publication of readings of individual poems.

Which poems will you be looking at?

Shakespeare's sonnets 29 and 30, Yeats's 'Tower' and Eliot's 'Prufrock'.
After an introductory essay, dealing with the need, and the method.

You've always admired 'Prufrock', haven't you?

It seems to me to be a very significant and very powerful narrative and
psychological success. And a real key to modern poetry.

Did it have an effect on your own work, do you think? A delayed effect?

I don't think so. It just seems to me to have cleared the deck for modern
poetry; in the first few lines, with the image of the 'patient etherised
upon a table', Edwardian and Victorian verse disappeared.

What other work will you be looking at?

'A Summer Night' by Auden, and some contemporary work. And I will
be trying Blake's 'The Mental Traveller'.

Blake's been a very strong, continuous influence.

More a fixation. I can't make full sense of 'The Mental Traveller', as I
think I have solved 'Prufrock', and can fully understand 'A Summer
Night'. There is a final stretch in 'The Mental Traveller' that I am sure I
will never figure out.

When you say 'solved' and 'stretch' what problem are you thinking about?

It is less a problem than a matter of detecting the structure – the plot and
full intention of the poem.

*Has Blake been an influence on the Peppercanisters as actual objects, in the
way that his books were art objects?*

Not really, at least not in terms of items with illustrations and special presentation. I return occasionally to the poems, touching base for a kind of psychic energy.

So in the readings then, is it a large book you are talking about? Will it be a Peppercanister?

It will. The first is ready, with the first few poems. Then hopefully a series, culminating in a full book.

That sounds like a departure from earlier Peppercanisters; *I know* The Dual Tradition *was a Peppercanister, but this seems something new.*

I am not certain of the final format, but it should have the actual texts, with the lines numbered. The readings will keep close to the text, with every detail followed and analysed. There will be no generalizations: no considerations of other poems, by the same poet or others, or other work of any kind; concentrating on the poem.

Would that be an ideal way for a reader to approach your own work, absolute concentration on the object at hand?

It should be the first step.

Your work has been very intent to know itself, and the relationships between the poems. What I mean is that much of your work is evolutionary. In 'Baggot Street Deserta' (Another September, 1958), *for example, you can see the connection between that poem and later poems, the obsession with blood, for instance, and the past, is present in many of your poems. To read your work fully, and with maximum attention, it seems that you need all of that in mind when approaching one of your poems.*

I don't think it is essential to keep it all in mind. . . Each poem should stand by itself. But with maximum attention in each case, the other things are a bonus. Relationships with earlier work are additional, not essential. There can be, and are, deliberate echoes, picking up earlier references.

In 'A Country Walk' (Downstream, 1962) *and* The Pen Shop (1997) *for example, 'the piercing company of women' is a deliberate echo.*

Yes.

'A Country Walk' and 'Tao and Unfitness at Inistioge on the River Nore' (One, 1974) *have a very close relationship.*

Yes, although the relationship there is more down through the actuality of the image – the flow of the river – than across from one poem to the other; each poem going down into the image and dealing with the same material. In the 'Inistiogue' poem it matters, for instance, that the tide and the flow cancel at a certain point.

Would you then consider that poem to be a deeper plumbing of an image than was present in 'A Country Walk'?

It is a different handling of the image. In 'A Country Walk' it appears strongly at the end – from a merely distant odour at the beginning of the poem – gathering up the energies of the poem, flowing underneath the bridge. In the 'Inistiogue' poem it's there throughout the action: at the close of the poem you have the local in his cot, in tune with the flow, handling the stream; whereas 'we' so to speak, are unfit. . . The locals with their salmon out of the past, out of the generations and the centuries.

What makes the 'locals' fit, and 'we' unfit?

Marginally unfit. The fact that we are aware of our apparent unfitness is important. 'Move, if you move, like water'; 'A brick, and its dust, fell'. Being aware of these instants of event is something external to the situation. Being aware of the process.

Is it a self-consciousness?

It is an awareness of the process: of the flow of the stream, of the decay of the building. For that instant.

And the 'locals' are not aware of this?

They are part of the process.

Is, therefore, part of what the poem, a poem, does, is it a trying to get back to that state, or is that state unattainable?

I think that the awareness is part of the unfitness. Now we are back with 'Prufrock'. He is the marginal case; at the end of the poem, he is not the hero; the sirens are singing, but not to him. But he is surviving. And he is recording. He is the artist and we are aware of his work.

Marginalisation, being at the edge, is that the state of artistic play since 'Prufrock'? Is that what you see the artist as being now?

I would feel that. It is only in rare and notable times that all the energies are in tune. As in ancient Ireland. Or in Elizabethan England, with major popular art. I don't know about Japan.

Could it ever be possible again?

I don't see why not.

What needs to come together for that to be possible?

I don't know. Lucky historical accident.

You have spoken of poetry as, along with other creative efforts – in the physical sciences and in philosophy – a contributor to understanding and the continual effort toward 'the ascendancy of the humane.' What is poetry's particular contribution to this effort? Is there a particularly Irish contribution?

It seems that poetry at its best, in the great exceptional times, can contribute a view of 'the process' as a whole. But even in the less fortunate times there is the valuable individual experience contributing the significant detail, together with a sense of the wholeness and importance of the process. At a time like the present, when religion has more or less vanished, poetry can almost act as a substitute.

The sciences are efforts towards understanding, working towards the same idea; an understanding of what is going on, of the process we are involved in. In most cases it is a matter of getting the detail clear. In certain major cases, as with Einstein or Darwin, you are getting the process clear. And in *The Origin of Species*, toward the end, Darwin approaches the state of poetry, responding to the process as a whole.

As to the Irish contribution, the nearest I can get is in the area of detail, like the early monastic poems. In the matter of understanding, I have used the best I could find in the book *Out of Ireland* (1987), quoting Giraldus Cambrensis on the Irish music of his time, 'the perfection of their art. . .' But I haven't made an orderly study of the prose.

So there's nothing essentially linking your work, or another Irish writer's work, or, let's say, Yeats and Beckett, or Yeats and ancient Irish poets?

With Yeats all I can see, in this context, is *A Vision*. And it seems to me to be an enormous, eccentric footnote to his own work, and no more than that. I have tried writing my own poem on the subject; to be published soon, in a new book of poems, along with the book of readings. It deals with the arts, sciences and religion – all of positive endeavour – functioning together. That poem will be preceded in the book by a poem of religious structure, a paganised wedding ceremony, of simple personal beginning, and an entry into the 'plot' as a whole.

When you say 'plot,' what are you indicating?

Evolution; the point of being born; making sense or no sense of existence.

The entire life process. . .

The point of the process – looking down as from an imagined viewpoint.

Asking why the effort continues to take place?

That is the question.

In Godhead (1999) you've used one of the old Irish poems (by the thirteenth-century poet Giolla Brighde Mac Con Midhe), which says 'All metre and mystery / touch on the Lord at last.' Is that significant?

I would ask: why a God would bother? With reality, under any circumstances? Reality having such drawbacks, why would a Creator – allegedly omnipotent, and exercising a sensible option – not decide against it?

Considering that 'something' has bothered, and we are faced with the consequences. . .

. . .we then accept the consequences. And the most we can hope to achieve is some kind of understanding. Looking into the process and making what sense we can; extracting order if possible; assembling some sort of meaningful structure to resist the effects of time; with the power to articulate, connecting the generations.

Is it a constant struggle against futility? Is futility always encroaching upon whatever it is that keeps us, keeps you, going?

There is the defensive retreat into significant detail. As with those early monastic, nature poems; the Irish contribution. Where, (although I may have questioned the Creator's basic impulse), I accept and value the memorable occasional detail.

You said once, to Seán Ó Riada, that you believed in God. Do you still?

From that imagined vantage point distant overhead, it would be very difficult. And yet there is a drive to make things happen down there. And when you push back into the past, into the first microsecond of time, physics and poetry intersect in a kind of religion.

In 'The Irish Writer' (1966) you wrote that the 'gapped, discontinuous, polyglot' tradition inherited by the Irish writer granted access to conditions of modernity faced by every contemporary writer. How have these conditions informed your own poetic development? Your development has, to an extent, been seen in national terms, with the early influence of English prosody being superseded by influences out of the Irish language, and by Joyce, for instance. What do you make of this reading?

I reject it. In fact the process has been a simply autobiographical one, dealing with the material as it presented itself. There was no question of nationalism – of Irish prosody ousting English; of Auden being displaced by Yeats or Joyce; of that kind of thing. My experience of poetry, until I found the poetry of Auden, was limited to memorizing poems in school, or parts of poems, with a few critical comments from nineteenth-century English writers. It was a meaningless exercise. Finding certain poems of Auden, after leaving school, I discovered the relationship between poetry and personal experience, and recognised that the expression of certain findings, in some way similar to Auden's, could be important to me. This was the beginning.

The Irish material came with suggestions from Liam Miller. His interest was primarily in fine printing, elegant books. He was looking for raw material. He suggested something out of the Old Irish, and we printed *The Breastplate of St Patrick* in 1954. The first prose translation, the same year, was *The Sons of Usnech*. I was struck by the quality of this – the oldest version of the Deirdre story – and by its superiority over the usual one, and I thought I would look closer at the rest of the Ulster stories. I was unprepared for the difficulties in the way of this mild curiosity. There were plenty of 'retellings' in the bookshops, but actual translations were scarce, and the *Táin Bó Cuailnge* was very badly represented. It seemed extraordinary that, for all the romanticised, fairy tale, versified, dramatised and bowdlerised versions of the Ulster cycle, there had never been a readable translation of the older version of the *Táin* as we first have it. So I undertook the work, and completed it as time offered.

Would the impulse behind An Duanaire (1981) *and the* New Oxford Book of Irish Verse (1986) *have been the same?*

T K Whitaker of the Department of Finance, where I worked for a while, gave the idea for the *Duanaire*, and the choice of poems was made by Seán Ó Tuama. I had the idea myself for a similar book for the early poetry, but couldn't find an editor agreeable for the same kind of work. I did it myself, and put together the *New Oxford Book of Irish Verse*: working on the principle that Irish poetry was important in both languages; that at certain times it functioned in Irish in certain ways; at other times in both English and Irish. It was a main aim of the *New Oxford Book* to give an idea of these two bodies of poetry and of the relationships between them. As to the translations, I used all my own translations, not thinking that the existing translations were adequate.

In what ways were they inadequate?

Frequently in being loose and not accurate. But mainly in not giving an adequate sense of the strength of the originals. They could be 'poetical,' without the intensity of the Irish.

What goal did you have as a translator, to carry that across into the English as much as possible?

To convey something like the force of the prose of the early *Táin* and of the poetry I had enjoyed working on with Ó Tuama for the *Duanaire*; that sense of the language being alive.

Can English manage to capture that aliveness?

Yes; and at its best I believe it's there in the translations. When I find myself checking for something in the anthologies, I have felt satisfied.

Is it still part of your creative process? Are the translations that you've done still part of something living within you?

Not really. I have moved on.

Goethe and Thomas Mann have been significant influences on your work. Could you speak a little about your initial attraction to German literature, and how these authors, and a figure such as Mahler, have informed your writing?

It was only a student interest. I was interested in Goethe and Kafka and Rilke, above all in Thomas Mann. All in translation. There was an opportunity once, to study the German language – in UCD; but there weren't enough students and it faded, and my studies in German faded. So I have only the slightest acquaintance with the language.

What was the first attraction to German literature, though? Was it something to do with the war, do you think?

Nothing like that. It was the music, above all; an abiding interest in German music. I find myself now – in one of my current efforts – writing a poem in thanks to Bach, for extricating order and presenting it as he does.

Your attraction to Bach is because of the order out of chaos that he achieved?

The manipulation of maximum detail, immense quantities of material in radiant order as in the great *Passions* and *Masses*. With the same skill in miniature, the power in delicacy, as in the cello suites. Similarly – although I have to allow for the fact of translation – with Thomas Mann, where you have the great structures, with control over detail. I was reading the Joseph stories, and Joyce, for the first time, and at the same time, with the same enthusiasm.

With Goethe you used part of the Faust story in Notes from the Land of the Dead, *the descent to the place of The Mothers. Was that something that developed later?*

Yes, and not necessarily from Goethe.

What role does dream and myth play in your poetry?

It can be shallow. As in 'Another September', at the close, with the dream figures bearing daggers and balances at the edge of sleep. It can be deeper, dealing with the creative act, and the psychic selection of significant imaginative material. . . Here, in the first part of the creative act, dream and myth are deeply involved. And one doesn't have much control in the selection of material; the material makes the selection.

How do you judge its value? Because it continually reappears in the imagination?

It presents itself as an opportunity, or a new project, and becomes the next fixation, from a source where you have no control. The material originates of itself, and you find yourself thinking in terms of the subconscious, the unconscious, the shared inherited unknown, and dealing with things of an importance impossible to explain: like why the moon is still important at night – it really isn't, but it always has been; children's stories; rhyme; religion; ceremony. Religion has disappeared, but ceremony has not. And the act of poetry: why you and I are prepared to spend our time talking about these things.

I am interested in the 'psychic selection of significant imaginative material.' How does 'significance' happen? When do you know that it's 'significant'?

By the fact that it presents itself, and keeps presenting itself, insistently, and by its relationships with other matter. I would have gambled against my writing religious poetry, but I find myself writing those religious poems. . .

To speak about a particular example. 'Hen Woman' (Notes from the Land of the Dead, 1973) *seems to be a fundamental psychic experience, an event from your own childhood, and you place it in relationship with the fundamental human psychic experience of the 'breaking of the egg.' Your poetry has found examples of these experiences in myth. I am thinking of the beetle in 'Hen Woman', which has a connection with the Egyptian scarab.*

And there is a related image at the end of the poem 'Chrysalides' (*Downstream*, 1962), where the young people on holiday, and on the threshold of maturity, find themselves faced with the realities of the future, in the brutal intensity of insect life. Another detail presenting itself unforgettably out of the process, out of ordinary daily experience. It would be hard to articulate the meaning, but it insists.

Has myth been a way to valorise your experience, to universalise these core experiences? Do you go looking for these things?

No. I have enough to handle as it is.

The effect of audience expectation, in the colonial situation for instance, and in the contemporary situation the loss of a public for poetry, have been concerns in both your poetry and in your critical writings. Could you elaborate on your idea of audience?

A poem, whatever else it is, is an act of communication, involving an audience. Communication is central – an audience completing an act of communication. In a faulty situation this relationship is lacking. But it is still necessary to project – communicating with an ideal audience. It is not enough to take notes – otherwise you keep a diary.

Is there a contradiction? The necessity to record, on the one hand, and the necessity for it not to be mere note taking?

The material needs to be adequately externalised. Organic embodiment of the material is the final phase of the creative function – of which the psychic selection of the material is the first. The embodiment needs to stand by itself, with the significant contents functioning in detail and form so that a reader can repeat the experience. But what kind of reader? Communication at what level; and to whom? There are no fixed standards or limits. Ideally, we are dealing with an ideal reader; possibly a projection of the poet's own creating self.

Like Yeats in 'The Fisherman', for example?

Yes.

Is the hope, therefore, that an audience will arise?

It will, if the work is adequate. I have considered the point in *The Dual Tradition*, dealing with modern Irish writing:

> . . .there is something in the direction [of the careers of Yeats and Joyce] that affects all modern Irish poets writing in English. These, producing a variety of poetry, occasionally of the highest kind, can find themselves faced with a conscious choice: whether, like Yeats at the beginning of his career, to address the work toward a responsive primary audience, but away from the area of experience; or, like Joyce, or Yeats in his later poetry, toward a primary audience sharing the facts of experience intimately with the writer – an audience that may not exist, an ideal audience, a projection of the self – allowing an actual audience to appear as and when it can.
> From early in the twentieth century writers other than Irish have been faced with the same choice, and with more involved than colonial or post-colonial issues. Addressing a responsive audience, one stays inside a world of 'traditional' art, an art primarily of communication. With the second choice one enters the world of modern art, an art primarily of exploration.

The balance between exploration and communication is difficult, and important. With matters of technique involved – of obscurity and tone and many other things. In dealing with Joyce: the impossibility of *Finnegans Wake*; the imbalance of manner over matter in some later chapters of *Ulysses*. It is a whole other subject.

What do you think of the critical response to your work?

I don't see it as having really begun. There are a few notable responses, seeing the point, in detail and as a whole: Maurice Harmon, Derval Tubridy, Brian John. Some writers abroad and in the USA. I have a sense of the critical responses of the present time dealing in careers more than in the work. That is why I have planned the book of readings – to encourage the close critical reading of individual texts.

What areas of your work do you think have been neglected?

I think I will let time be the judge of that – and stay at the work.

In 'Downstream', in 'Tao and Unfitness at Inistioge on the River Nore', and via Mahler's Das Lied von der Erde, *there are a number of references to Chinese poetry and philosophy. Could you speak a little about your knowledge of Chinese, and Japanese, literature?*

I have to confess that it is virtually nil. Not going beyond a few vague usages and a sense of what is involved. With the German also, the background is not as profound as might seem. I think the poetry is more predatory than it is given credit for; just taking what it needs.

It's an extraordinarily allusive body of work, so the tendency is to perhaps look at the sources and see this enormously predatory, you call it, imagination at work, seizing these things, and there are tentacles spreading out everywhere and you go after one tentacle, and another. . .

It is certainly not scholarly: that would be impossible. But it is this same element which keeps cropping up: of the detail and the whole. Of an overall process functioning on the basis of detail. The detail needing to be precise. If the detail is not distinct and reliable, the rest does not matter. In fact, the concept of the process is expendable; if the detail is adequate, that is sufficient.

When you speak of 'detail' what would be an example? Is detail to do with a word. . .?

A word, the capture of an instant: 'A brick, and its dust, fell.' Or the instant at the end of 'Tao and Unfitness' where the man in the flat cot with the fish moves out of the dusk – with his companions out in the darkness, and his ghost companions in the past – and passes back in again. That matters.

So getting that instant right. . .

. . .getting that paddle touching the water right is what matters. If you don't get that right the entire notion of process doesn't matter. It all hinges on precision of data.

This is an edited version of an interview which first appeared in
the *Journal of Irish Studies*, Vol. XIX.

Thomas Kinsella

TWO SONNETS BY WILLIAM SHAKESPEARE

SONNET 29

When, in disgrace with fortune and men's eyes,
I all alone beweep my outcast state,
And trouble deaf heaven with my bootless cries,
And look upon myself, and curse my fate,
Wishing me like to one more rich in hope,
Featured like him, like him with friends possess'd,
Desiring this man's art, and that man's scope,
With what I most enjoy contented least;
Yet in these thoughts myself almost despising,
Haply I think on thee, – and then my state,
Like to the lark at break of day arising
From sullen earth, sings hymns at heaven's gate;
For thy sweet love remember'd such wealth brings,
That then I scorn to change my state with kings.

First quatrain

Lines 1 - 2   Noting that the syntax is suspended with the word; and
registering the open scene: a condition of isolation and
shame, rejected by circumstance and by mankind.
Regarded with ignominy in the eyes of men; his own
eyes pouring tears.

Line 3   The rejection equated with the expulsion from Eden.
The private weeping now an outcry, complaining – and
looking – toward Heaven; Heaven deaf; the cries unavailing.

Line 4   The cries – and the regard of the eyes – turned back with
curses upon the self.

A first quatrain of emotional and sensual extremes. Intense in
imagery, so that the word 'disgrace' reads as the actual deprivation of
grace, and the word 'outcast' as the act of casting out; the eye
imagery strong in line 4 so that the outcast – disgraced in men's eyes
in line 1 – is disgraced in his own eyes also.

Second quatrain

> Lines 5 - 8: The synatx still suspended. The basis for the emotions
> of the first quatrain; the standards against which the complaints
> are measured: others more gifted by circumstance – one more
> gifted with looks, another with ease of friendship; one colleague
> with a particular technical skill, another with a range of theme,
> so that even in his chosen calling he is unsatisfied.

The second quatrain, without imagery, empties the sonnet of
the extremes of the first.

Third quatrain

> The extremes of the first quatrain, and their removal in the
> second, prepare for a third quatrain of dramatic effect.
>
> Line 9: The solutions begin: of syntax ('Yet'); and of the
> emotional crisis ('almost').
>
> Line 10: The happy accident ('Haply') occurs on a memory of
> the beloved – the two previous sonnets having dealt with the
> pain of the beloved's absence –, initiating a change in the outcast
> state. This is the second use of 'state' in a rhyming position,
> readying it for a change of meaning.
>
> Line 11: His state, rising like a lark – from nowhere, out of the
> dark into the light – with tiny explosive effect (a small richness of
> dentals and three small 'k's in a setting of open vowels). . .
>
> Line 12: . . .gives voice to the outcast world. The voice is tiny, and
> Heaven's gate remains shut, but the voice is singing hymns and
> no longer complaining. The imagery of the first quatrain
> restored, transfigured.
>
> Lines 13 - 14: Ending with a couplet of lowered intensity: the
> problem solved; the argument proven. And a third use of 'state',
> the meaning enhanced by 'Kings' and the introduction of the
> idea of wealth.

The concept of wealth is treated in the next sonnet

SONNET 30

When to the sessions of sweet silent thought
I summon up remembrance of things past,
I sigh the lack of many a thing I sought,
And with old woes new wail my dear time's waste:
Then can I drown an eye, unused to flow,
For precious friends hid in death's dateless night,
And weep afresh love's long-since-cancell'd woe,
And moan the expense of many a vanish'd sight:
Then can I grieve at grievances foregone,
And heavily from woe to woe tell o'er
The sad account of fore-bemoaned moan,
Which I new pay as if not paid before.
But if the while I think on thee, dear friend,
All losses are restored, and sorrows end.

First quatrain

> Lines 1 - 2: The image of a judicial assembly established, in an atmosphere of pleasant nostalgia. Memories called up from the past for silent scrutiny.

> Line 3: Nostalgia turning to melancholy, quiet, – but sighing, no longer silent, with the memory of things sought in the past, and not achieved.

> Line 4: The memory sharpening, the sigh increasing to a wail, with the renewed painful awareness of things once possible and let pass, or achieved and squandered; key words 'wail' and 'waste'. The judicial assembly reduced, now, to the one.

Second quatrain

> Line 5: With the solitary, sharpened memory – and accompanying the wail –, tears that had flowed once for the loss, and ceased, flow again as though for the first time. . .

> Line 6 . . .for the loss of precious friends lost in death's timeless dark;

> Lines 7 - 8: weeping once again for the grief that had healed in a past love, and lamenting again the cost, or loss, of past experience.

Beginning with 'deare' and 'waste' in line 4; and developing through 'precious', 'dateles', 'canceld' and 'expence'; the idea of loving friend-ship has combined with that of accountancy and wealth. The woe for lost friendship is a debt due, and presented again for payment – dateless, that was thought cancelled. Key words are 'woe' and 'moan'.

Third quatrain

Lines 9-12: The full account presented for payment. The uncancelled woes lamented and counted over heavily, as by an accountant or clerk, and paid again as if for the first time, with the repeated excessive open vowel sounds of 'woe' from line 7 and 'moan' from line 8.

Lines 13 and 14: Tensions of sense and sound solved in a simple couplet. All losses, and sorrows, made good by the thought of the dear friend. After the excessively articulated mourning of lines 10 to 12 it is difficult to articulate line 13 without exercising the muscles of a smile.

Alice Lyons

THE FUGITIVE ELECTRIC OF YOU

August Kleinzahler, *The Strange Hours Travellers Keep* (Faber, 2004), £9.99.

August Kleinzahler's style is natty – no shabby corduroy blazers with
suede elbow patches on this poet's language. Sharkskin, more like it. Or
moiré. Shimmering and shifting colour, his poetry chameleons up and
down the scales: from formal BBC diction to crass 'Joisey' shyster spiels,
from the ethereal to the scatological, from reverie to bitter cynicism.
Chord structure is central to the way his poems are built. And the more
complex tonalities within one poem, the fuller and truer Kleinzahler's
sound rings out. Both the title of the current collection, *The Strange
Hours Travellers Keep* (nominated for the Forward Prize in 2004), and the
epigraphs obviously focus our attention on the theme of travel. But,
frankly, Kleinzahler's poetry has always created the sensation of being on
the move.

It's not the external fact of travel, but the internal transformation it
offers that is Kleinzahler's focus. Travel gets us off the hamster wheel of
everyday oblivion. It forces us to live further out into our nerve endings.
Perceptions are heightened. Strange hours invite us to observe what we
normally shut out. Dawn is framed in the oval airplane window, a
throbbing orange orb of marvel. Travel is a 'willed indolence' ('Rx for
S'), and Kleinzahler's point is that it can wake us up to the world again
after the deep sleep brought on by productivity and the Work Ethic.

The settings of the poems here will be mostly familiar to readers of
Kleinzahler's previous books. There's the East Coast-West Coast volley
between the 'pastels and hills' of San Francisco and the 'warrens and fast-
nesses' of Brooklyn. There's a paean to Interstate Highway 35 in Austin,
Texas. The collage-like 'Montreal' – a familiar backdrop in his earlier
poems – re-works, in part, material from his 1978 collection, *A Calendar of
Airs*. Berlin, where Kleinzahler did a stint at the American Academy, is a
new poem location.

Kleinzahler is a most visual poet. The space of his poems constantly
shifts from close up to panorama. Film lingo, suggestions for soundtracks,
references to photography, painting, installation, architecture are woven
through the work. His visual sense swaggers. One thinks of Scorcese or
Cartier-Bresson's American photos. Kleinzahler composes with a sense of
vivid colour and dramatic intensity as in Scorcese's films. Or when his
palette is in black-and-white, it employs the measured tonal control of
Cartier-Bresson.

An example of such tonal range in *The Strange Hours Travellers Keep* is a poem set nowhere more exotic than the speaker's home, where he's returning after a long journey. The poem, 'Back' is drawn in grisaille, achieving a quality of restraint that builds the refined emotion the poem requires. The poem grapples with the heightened sensations of strangeness and familiarity that sift through the traveller when what was once like a second skin is now eerily foreign: 'How familiar it all slowly becomes: / a photograph / still murky in its chemical bath / a tune or aroma / not quite placed but close in the mind, / and then, yes, ah, that, my my. . .'
The poem comes into focus gradually and delicately picks out moments of clarity – 'a seagull on a piling'; 'or the garlic press / found at last behind the vinegars and pastes' – in an overall wash of 'cool, silvered air'. Lines such as 'So many people have passed through in my absence', or 'Away for so long I'm other than I was', which could sound vapid elsewhere, achieve the correct weight of poignancy in the overall weight-lessness of the poem.

It's in this mode of compressed tonalities that one senses the elasticity of the range of sounds, colours and textures Kleinzahler can achieve. And as if to clobber us with the notion, this lovely Corot of a poem is sandwiched next to 'Balling at 50', which is drawn with the sexy clumsiness of a Robert Crumb cartoon. But that's part of this poet's approach. He never stays in any one mode too long. Reading through this collection is like visiting an amusement park, say, Palisades Park, down the road from where Kleinzahler grew up in New Jersey. One poem might be a Ferris wheel to lift you high up into the ethers, offering enchanting views of the Hudson and the New York skyline. But in the next one, you're thrown into the 'Cyclone of Death' where you're stuck to the wall by centrifugal force. Then the floor falls out.

American architect Robert Venturi's 1966 book on the urban landscape, *Complexity and Contradiction in Architecture*, shuns the orthodoxy of modernism and calls for a re-enchanting look at the 'messy vitality' of American cities while retaining the best of the modernist contribution. Kleinzahler's aesthetic chimes nicely with this. *The Strange Hours Travellers Keep* is full of the visual, verbal, and vocal contrasts that Kleinzahler has catalogued from the beginning. He loves, for example, to set the yucky against the lovely, as in 'cat jism and perfume' ('Montreal'). Or he'll glide from *King James Bible*-style diction ('You ask, Aristippus, and I tell you') into the Blues ('grinding and tossing like to break your back in two') in a short distance ('Epistle XIV').

Another 'epistle' to a friend who lives in the country is really an extended rant on why the country bores Kleinzahler, and the poetry makes this evident. You just don't get the clash and complexity that drive Kleinzahler's polychrome – too much sameness, and it's all green.

But the birdsong for me, right up there with Bartók and Monk,
is never straight up but part of a mix—footsteps, traffic
fountains, shouts—that beggar Cage and Stockhausen.
Accident, contingency: it's city nature, Maecenas, that's for me,
not those endless manured fields, lowing cattle and whatever
sheep do

In 'A History of Western Music' we travel to Ireland, where its 'famously tragic' and 'tortured' history are italicised and the scene is heavingly scored with Mahler's fifth Symphony. It's interesting, if a bit predictable, to see how a trip to Glendalough and St Kevin's bed (with the memory of Heaney's poem lurking in the glen) is handled. 'A haunted place', the female guide warns, and you can feel Kleinzahler winding up for an anti-romantic knuckleball, which he delivers. Who appears in this bucolic, reverent setting? Liberace, his sequin outfit producing a halo-like effect.

'Epistle XIV' playfully bats around a sober notion that runs through the collection: that what it takes to live a life dedicated to the art of poetry is deeply at odds with the nine-to-five world of contemporary life, or even the achievement oriented universe of the 'Po Biz' – 'the rag trade', as the speaker in the poem calls it: 'wholesale, plenty of volume. There's the action / steady, too, and regular hours: / push, and push hard enough, you've got it made. / Not like this wretched, unforgiving game / where you can sit around for months sniffing / at the air like a patient in a convalescent ward / for mentals; knackered, reamed, a source of amusement for all the neighbors to see / . . .In the end, what it comes down to is appetite – / the enforced idleness, the solitude: / nothing, hectacres of nothing, litanies of nothing on microfiche. . .'

One gets the sense that Kleinzahler is quite adept at pissing people in the 'Po Biz' off. 'The Art Farm' is a case in point. It's the latest expression of his distaste for the creative writing industry that strangles the soul of poetry in the United States today. What is worth remarking on is not so much the fun he pokes at artist retreats and the 'fructifying' experiences they provide. It is the passion for the medium that underlies Kleinzahler's rages that is notable and central to the ethic of his poetry. He's got nothing but snarling anger towards those who 'position themselves' to do their art.

There's an essay tacked onto the end of Faber's collection of Kleinzahler's earlier poetry, Live at the Hong Kong Nile Club, which amplifies all this. It's well worth reading and makes the point, echoed in The Strange Hours Travellers Keep, that academia is 'poisonous' to the life of a writer. As in the poems, the prose style is full of verve and feeling. Opinions are pitched at high volume. Not the writing of a sober, distant, judicial mind. It's much more hot-headed and passionate with the attendant delights and furies of such a temperament. See also Kleinzahler's hilarious piece in *Poetry* (April 2004) on Garrison Keillor, 'No Antonin Artaud With The Flapjacks, Please'. Since its publication, the letters to the editor section in *Poetry* has been all het-up for months.

Kleinzahler ends this collection with 'The Tartar Swept', a poem about a ferocious people living by their wits, 'for whom a roof and four walls is like unto a grave.' It's a cascade of images of destruction, beauty, cunning and strangeness arriving 'at the gates of Christendom.' Not a bad metaphor for the untamed, subversive force of art.

So what exactly do Kleinzahler's poems capture in the net of their formidable technical acuity? What is at the heart of this poetry? To my mind, poems such as 'Back' point the way. They distil and refine the poet's most resonant visions, capturing a fugitive moment, like an astonishing musical performance that rings out and then disperses into the ether.

It is in this sense that Kleinzahler's best work is evidence of the world having passed through his 'instrument', 'the electric of you' as he calls it in the opening poem of a previous collection, *Red Sauce, Whiskey and Snow* – the unique combo of perceptual and sensory filters that he tilts into the wind. His most penetrating poems have a heightened, almost psycho-pharmaceutical reality. They make a vertiginous record of an unleashed receptivity to raw experience. The protagonist of the title poem of his previous collection, *Green Sees Things in Waves*, is crippled by perceptual hypersensitivity (a few too many acid trips), but the recently woken-up speaker in 'Hyper-Berceuse: 3 a.m.' in the current collection stays on this side of sanity:

> The ceiling and walls are star maps
> Breathing, alive
> Those aren't stars, darling
> that's your nervous system
> Nanna didn't take you to planetariums like this
> Go on, touch
> Lovely, isn't it
> Like phosphorus on Thule lake
> Sweet summer midnights
> Shimmery, like applause under the skin

Apogee – that is the search engine of this poetry, a perfect moment of pure, sensate experience. It rings out and then vanishes. The work is peppered with encounters with such perfection. Along the way, Kleinzahler notes the garbage, the nuttiness, the bestiality as well – constituent parts of the messy vitality that lures him.

Fred Johnston

RIPPED FROM THE FAMILIAR

John Montague, *Drunken Sailor* (Gallery Press, 2004), €11.40.
Ed. by Thomas Dillon Redshaw, *Well Dreams: Essays on John Montague*
(Creighton University Press, 2004), €15.

One might suggest that Montague is a better poet than Heaney, a poet to
whom he's always been favourable. Identified always as an Ulster Poet,
the jacket blurb to his latest collection at the age of seventy-five describes
him as a doyen of this tribe and doesn't mention Heaney; like Padraic
Fiacc, another Ulster Poet, Montague was born in the United States.
Since so many Ulstermen emigrated there, and a fair number of
American presidents came of Ulster stock, the exchange is reasonable.
    Montague's position in Irish poetry generally is complex. Ulster-ness
was rather thrust upon him at a very young age; born in Brooklyn in
1929, he was reared in County Tyrone. In some ways that has made him
an *orphelin du pays*; we are hardly surprised that he lived in France, has
translated the work of Francis Ponge, lives occasionally in France still
and is more openly European than most of his generation. He has dug
deeply into the Ulster and more wholly Irish soil from his earliest
collections: Dolmen Press published his *Patriotic Suite* in 1966, and his
involvement with traditional music, well-acknowledged, led him to
dedicate the little book with its woodcuts to Seán Ó Riada. The first part
of the sequence, 'The Lure', is decidedly more European in style than
the kinds of poetry being written in Ireland at the same time. The card-
poem, 'A New Siege', from 1970, was dedicated to Bernadette Devlin.
Perhaps a tad cosier was the issue of The Dolmen magazine which,
under his editorship, carried the beginnings of *Langrishe, Go Down*, by
Aidan Higgins, and Richard Murphy's 'The Cleggan Disaster'; while at
the same time allowing Montague an essay on *The Deserted Village* and a
review of his just-published *Poisoned Lands*. Yet Montague seems, amidst
all of these political and cultural ruminations, always to have been
obsessed – too strong a word? – by notions of ageing, of moving beyond
a Rubicon of some kind; as early as 1979, *The Leap*, published also by
Gallery, contains a poem entitled 'Crossing':

> 'Age should bring its wisdom
> but in your fragrant presence
> my truths are one. . .'

Montague excels at love poetry, Heaney arguably shies away from it. Both poets investigate their identities and that of a place and a time; the non-American-by-birth was more clearly favoured by the academic establishment, especially in the United States.

Montague's new collection seems to be both reminder of the solid lyric poet and the conscientious statement-maker; the Muse man and the young-old purveyor of wisdom. In four parts, like a designed piece of music, the collection also and poignantly opens with a reference to Montague's Brooklyn boyhood and the Cork identity he espoused for so long. The mortality thing rears its head then with a quote from the Poet Formerly Known as Hokusai (I'm not joking) in old age.

The first section poems are mirrors held up to a scattery but recognisable psyche, full of wildness and natural danger which engages symbols such as hags and currachs, fast cars and the ghost of Roethke. This is Montague as was, answering something in the flagrant energetic upside-down-ness of the Irish spirit, while giving us a glimpse of Europe's drunken shore:

> . . .her drunken lover
> clambers out, blinking,
> to pee furiously
> into the festive sea.   – 'Last Resort, Normandy'

The second section doesn't muck about so much and gets down to the business of taking poems, old and new, from the Irish, playing with form and investigating ghoulish local myth, where two lads putting their heads on a railway track die 'like Elizabethans'. All history is local in one sense of other. 'The Deer Trap' is a mythic 'transformation' prose-poem (Francis Ponge is the French master of this form, which he calls *'Proèmes'*; Montague the love-poet would know, however, that Ponge wrote *'Je doute que le véritable amour comporte du désir, de la ferveur, de la passion.'*) And there's a nod to the late Kathleen Raine; the mythic value of Mount Ventoux and the area of the Luberon, not terribly far from where I'm writing this. Europe-as-myth? He even seems to think that Ireland, somehow, can be saved by 'remembering' myth, and in this he becomes inordinately, and perhaps naively, Yeatsian:

> Observe the giant machines trundle over
> this craggy land. . .
>
> [. . .]
>
> . . .But see, the rushes rise again, by stealth
> tireless warriors, on the earth's behalf.   – 'Demolition Ireland'

No, sadly, money and the money-men will prevail, as Yeats knew and wrote; we have inherited his greasy till and fumble in it delightedly.

The third section deals rather head-on, at least for a few yards, with Montague's childhood, a religion-dismayed place, and moves on to short poems meditating about death or the dead in one way or other. Morbid, if we didn't know that Montague does this and often; it even contains a poem called 'Grave Song.'

The final long-poem section is a drive through Ireland to rediscover its myth-mad, superstitious heart, its wells and stories, so personal and heart-felt. Montague's poetry has made a similar journey before in *The Rough Field*. We end up near Sligo, where, almost certainly, the bones of Yeats do not lie, and with a glance back at the 'tale told by an idiot' notion: '. . .and all this never happened, or was told by a doting man?' No doter, Montague, whose poetical treks and explorations are even more relevant in an Ireland who does not know whether she's fish or fowl, and in some cases prefers simply to be foul.

Many books of essays on poets should be subtitled *Here Be Monsters*. Heavily academicised, they have often rendered a poet unreadable or incomprehensible, where previously he or she had been a joy to read; there is, for some, a thin line between diagnosing with the tips of one's fingers and chopping up for the coroner's block. The truth is that the process of creating a poem is a mystery and probably unexaminable. Dedicated also to Seán Lucy, one hopes this book brings more readers to Montague. But poetry read with the head is one thing, and poetry read with the heart quite another.

Twenty-three essay writers appear here, a dusting of poets among them; Montague's work is examined in very readable depth, thankfully; Redshaw reminds us that Montague was initially praised for his prose fiction; more healthy light is thrown on what Montague did to introduce Heaney as a poet to the scene, Daniel Tobin's essay drags in Freud and odd-sounding German words which I cannot forgive; Liam Ó Dochartaigh reminds us of the important and not-to-be forgotten poets' tour, 'The Planter and the Gael', undertaken by the roots-seeking Montague and the all-too-damned-certain-where-he-stood-regionally John Hewitt, and there is valuable insight into Gaelic ideas in Montague's *The Rough Field*; Richard Greaves and Michael Parker are both right and illuminating to suggest that Montague is compelled 'by an increasingly disturbing public narrative to engage in more complex ways with an ideology and history he had inherited. . .', and they suggest how he accomplished this; Elizabeth Grubgeld has a fascinating essay on how Montague's work deals with, or fails properly to deal with, the maternal, childhood and by extension, women, and his methods of mourning; Dillon Johnston is founder of Wake Forest University Press, which publishes and has

published some other Gallery Press poets, including Montague, in the
United States, if I recall correctly; Richard Bizot suggests Montague's
debt to Joyce.

All in all, a decent and clarifying collection of essays which, one
would hope, projects John Montague's work into a new and more direct
light. Yet it's hard for this reviewer – who experienced the same – to
escape the notion of Montague as a child ripped from the familiar and
plunged into a chronic search for identity, a search which ends in no
definite country but one imagined and constantly recreated, and which
transcends growing up or growing old. Words, legends, history, myth are
merely other types of toys; what we are creating is a hearth-world of our
own, from which we can never, until a very real end, be separated again.

Michael S Begnal

STRANGLED FROM THE MOON

Alan Jude Moore, *Black State Cars* (Salmon Poetry, 2004), €12.

Very few countries are famous for their poets the way Ireland is, so to be
an Irish poet brings with it certain expectations. What sets Alan Jude
Moore apart is that he subverts these expectations at every turn. He is
decidedly urban and internationalist and strives always (like Pound) for
the new. *Black State Cars*, Moore's first collection, is therefore a bold and
ambitious statement of purpose, showcasing an original voice. Moore
has a pan-European approach in terms of his poetics, and is just as likely
to take a cue from Apollinaire or Montale or Lorca as he is from Yeats or
Kavanagh.

None of which is to say that he is free from the weight of history – in
fact it is one of his biggest subjects – but he treats it differently than other
contemporary Irish poets. In 'Heading into darkness outside Athlone',
for example, he writes 'History coils around my leg / and begs', and
refers scornfully to those 'externalised historical centres' (but no doubt
paid for with EU funds!) In 'Berlin', history becomes a metaphor for a
relationship: 'Arm in arm, alone like stars. / Berlin is against itself again.'
Relationships are another of Moore's big subjects, but again he deals
with it atypically. This is a poetry of ideas. Ideas which he connects to the
particulars of a life, as in 'I do not remember':

> I do not remember how I held you,
> now we are both broken free. I do not remember
> those moments of freedom between us. And
> I do not remember the slow death of our time,
> stations washed in a little rain, hallways bleeding
> history.

He is not particularly 'political,' but he is conscious of the fact that
nothing and no one exists without a context.

Moore does tend to be analytical, however, but without sacrificing
poetry. That is, his writing is clear and direct without being reduced to
prose – it is not that stripped. He has a gift for offbeat description ('She
looks like she lives in other people's rooms', 'Canal Bridge'), for the
offbeat image ('By the church where you cried / I saw the sun bleed to
death. . .', 'Black State Cars'), and for a myriad of surrealistic similes
('our future / like a cuckold, hanging strangled from the moon', 'The

Hand'). If the term 'modernist' can be used to describe a *style* of writing, as opposed simply to a temporal development in the history of Western literature, then Moore is most definitely a modernist writer, an heir to the spirit of James Joyce (*Ulysses* rather than *Finnegans Wake*), Flann O'Brien and Thomas MacGreevy. He does not quite verge on the scientific strategies of certain other contemporary non-mainstream Irish poets like Randolph Healy, though. He is less concerned with linguistics in and of itself than he is with making language express the idiosyncrasy of his own experience and conception. There is still the lyric 'I', however ruthless it may be.

Some of the most interesting poems in *Black State Cars* are those which deal with Ireland as it is today. Contemporary Ireland is a society in transition, still searching for its identity, sometimes embarrassing itself horribly. For Moore at least, the old paradigms are no longer sufficient:

> It has been beaten into shape;
> we find ourselves drinking
> to the banging of bodhráns
> and the rattle of banjos.
> (As if it was meant to be
> like this long ago.)

> [. . .]

> It spreads from the middle out
> to the edge, selling Irish Things
> that would not be claimed
> in any lost and found.
> A Celtic cross on a bog muck base,
> a jacket made of dried-up grass. . .   – 'Smithfield'

A poem trading in the ridiculousness of something risks becoming ridiculous itself, but Moore pulls it off. Even better is the short piece 'Perversion at the Winding Stair Bookshop & Café', a snapshot of Dublin at the death of the twentieth century, in which the poet writes of 'Che Guevara credit cards' while missing 'the alcoholics / The five in the morning bullshit. . .' His realization is that 'I have no favourite woman and no mother tongue'. Moore's relationship to the Irish language is problematic at best. He is not against it *per se* (he is not one of those anti-Gaelic reactionaries), but for him – a Dubliner looking to the Continent rather than to the West of Ireland – it would be an affectation (never mind that, for many, the Irish language is a viable and authentic mode of communication). In 'The Fountain', a poem set in Galway (tellingly, 'I don't know where I am'), he deals specifically with the question of personal identity: 'Like a foreigner, or a spy, I conspire to spot my own kind. / Neither of us really care. Or say anything much about it.' Going further, he writes,

> I can still say only what I am not. Mumbling Montale,
> that one phrase in Italian. Like any good forgetful night,
>
> find a friend who talks more than you. Even *as Gaeilge*;
> you can pretend to listen. You might even believe it yourself. . .

So, Irish, but not bound to country. There are also powerful poems set in Rome ('Basilica'), Moscow ('Prospekt Mira'), etc.

And as the national paradigm is not sufficient for Moore, neither are the old poetic models. The result is a style that hints more at what Irish poetry could become than what it has been. Which is not to imply that a certain type of poetic nationalism might not also be reformulated for the new century – as indeed a few are already in the process of doing. But Moore represents another kind of writer who feels himself outside of all that, and both positions are equally valid. What is necessary in either case is to seek new forms and new language in order to express new ideas and experience. Moore is doing so, and that is what makes *Black State Cars* an important and essential collection.

Barra Ó Seaghdha

ROUGH GUIDE TO NEW IRISH POETRY

Ed. by Selina Guinness, *The New Irish Poets* (Bloodaxe, 2004), £10.95.

Editors of anthologies of contemporary poetry have a dream as the big day approaches: a calm lead-in, no medical complications, tears of joy on all sides as the perfect baby emerges, acclamation and congratulatory cards as the little darling is shown to the world. The reality is often different: strangers criticising the nose, the feet and every other feature; other parents holding their own babies in the air and proclaiming their superiority; sneers at the choice of name; dark hints about the real parentage. We remember some of the battles over the anthologies of Muldoon, Kinsella, Fallon/Mahon, Field Day; Selina Guinness, editor of *The New Irish Poets*, must have known from the beginning that she was embarking on a difficult project which would leave no-one entirely satisfied. And of course no-one is. Writers, editors, academics and critics approach an anthology differently from uninvolved readers. For the person who picks up a copy of this book in Glasgow or Bradford, it is the poems themselves, rather than the editorial back-story and apparatus, that will speak or not speak. This is something that reviewers, too, need to keep in mind.

For this particular review, the book was first read, then set aside and (after a lapse of time) read backwards. The result was a stronger sense of what the poems and poets had in common – and, frequently, a sense that they had too much in common. There is no formula for producing poetry and it is most certainly not a case of installing the latest poetic software and hitting the appropriate buttons. Poetry emerges where it will, to the bafflement of those who think they can control it. It is surprising, nonetheless, that – in a country which has undergone striking social, political and spiritual transformation, which is open to the worldwide swirl and ebb of economic and media energies, and in which it is difficult to remain unaware of the babble of competing languages that characterise the art, literature, music and architecture of the last hundred years – there is so much consensus on the language of poetry in Ireland.

Judging from the poets gathered in this anthology, at least, what is the nature of this consensus? Many poems recount or reshape the personal experience and memories of the poets. Many move towards the delivery of a perception or, in certain cases, a relatively straightforward message. Many remain very close to the language of standard literary prose. Many poems scarcely vary in tone or voice. Many poems sit rather slackly within the stanza shapes they adopt and have a limited aspiration towards rhythmic or musical energy or distinctiveness. Many poems are syntactically straightforward.

This is not an anthology of the best poems written in the last ten years by Irish writers; it is a selection of poems by a selection of writers who emerged over the last decade. Given that many poets are quickly forgotten, that many who survive do so through a handful of poems, it would be a miracle if an anthology such as this contained poems of uniform excellence or if an individual reader found the majority of the poems satisfying.

One reader's impressions, then.

In Vincent Woods's work, there is a surprising variety of voice and approach; some poems do not come off, but 'The Asylum is Water. . .' achieves a density of feeling and detail ('Sky softens, animal colours streak all tense, / make mute all things but stain. / Across the bay the sea is stone / swimming in light.') Something similar occurs in the case of Aidan Rooney-Céspedes: some varied and loosely energetic poems and then, with 'Rainbarrel', a subject that seems to concentrate all the poet's resources and to send his imagination spinning.

The poet-critics associated with *Metre* magazine show no trace of a house-style. Justin Quinn's bright ironies and sense of detail make for effective poems; in 'I wake early. . .', however, he reaches for something richer in substance. Caitríona O'Reilly can enter into a subject successfully ('Octopus', 'A Brief History of Light') but there is a tendency for the energy to leak out of poems at the close: '. . .Bats / utterly wrapped up in themselves.'('A Lecture Upon the Bat'); 'brought the masonry of childhood definitively tumbling / confirming even my worst imaginings' ('To the muse'). On the evidence of this selection, David Wheatley's poetry is nowhere near as impressive as his critical writings. With the possible exception of the brief 'Verlaine Dying', the language is either flat, 'Once I walked all night and called it quits / somewhere miles from home, then caught the first / bus back. What mattered was being lost', from 'Autumn, the Nightwalk, the City, the River'; or flatly ironic – as in the 'Sonnets to James Clarence Mangan': 'My fate is in the hands of Dial Your Stars, / off-peak rates, I'm pinning all my hope / on Tarot One-to-One and Live Feng Shui.'

Both Maurice Riordan and Cathal McCabe are drawn to intricacies of form, but with differing results. In McCabe's case, the accomplishment of the formal task he sets himself is not accompanied by any linguistic or imaginative energy. Maurice Riordan's 'Caisson' – more than other poems of his, and more than almost any other poem in the anthology – shows what happens when syntax and thought hesitate and unfold together, and how an astringent music can be created when an idea pushing forward towards definition is restrained and strengthened by the shape of the line. This is how it begins:

If light, then, could part the carbon lattices

Or: our ears were like bats' — but so enhanced,
So threaded into the brain, we saw the world

As noise: the tearing of skin, or keratin,
Hand abrading hand, would reverberate

Along 'the hearing bones' and be resolved
As line, texture, colour. . .

This is a poem to be read and re-read. What, then, of 'Hats' by Paula Cunningham? 'This year I tried on voices just like hats. // Whore hat / Bored hat / Life's a fucking chore hat / Tore hat / Sore hat/ Never bloody score hat / Can't take any more hat. . .' Read aloud by the author, this may wow an audience, but it is more a performing score than a poem to be read by the solitary reader. In Britain and increasingly in Ireland, poets are coming to depend on public readings. Is it too soon to judge the effect this is having on the tone and texture of the work? Tom French's is an interesting case. His poems are generally no more written for performance than those of any other writer here, but his 'Pity the Bastards' seems to call out for performance. Gearóid Mac Lochlainn has multiple identity as musician/performer/poet. A poem like 'Na hEalaíontóirí' is quite vivid on the page: 'B'anáil muid, comhréir, stad, / línte scaoilte, / teanga bhláth na n-airní / ag cleitearnach go suaimhneach / idir iall oscailte an leoin / is mearbhall mire/ an luascáin eitilte.'

It is not possible here to comment on every contributor. There are writers who have established their own imaginative worlds – Jean Bleakney, Celia de Fréine, Sam Gardiner, Vona Groarke, Kerry Hardie and so on. Of some – Conor O'Callaghan, Katie Donovan, Mary O'Donoghue – it might be said that they have settled a little too comfortably within its borders. There are writers whose promise intrigues or who are difficult to categorise. Yvonne Cullen is one of the latter, her work ranging from the musicality of 'For Letters', through what seems the elusively confessional approach of 'Not a Letter' or 'Signals', to the impersonal lyricism of 'Memorial'. Nick Laird's voice is very assured, but the few poems here are not enough to show whether he is not also being spoken by others. Of one young voice, it is probably too early to speak. Leanne O'Sullivan has a poetic sensibility. What it develops into, time will tell. Whether development is really helped by early promotion, which can so easily slide towards hype, is open to question.

It is very common for reviews of anthologies to descend into what-aboutery. Selina Guinness cannot be reproached for the choices she has made from within a particular writer's work. But there are other choices which almost invite what-aboutery. The title itself raises questions. What is meant by the term 'New Irish Poets'? The Introduction states that the anthology collects the work of 33 poets who published their first collection 'in or after 1993.' Presumably, the editorial work was largely carried out by 2003, making this an anthology of the new voices of the decade 1993-2003. The book itself was published in 2004, meaning that the decade referred to in the blurb is not quite the editor's decade. This slight shift will aggravate the irritation of writers unlucky enough to have had their first work published in 1992, for example. The editor situates the poets in the context of social and political development in the 1990s without showing why a line should be drawn at 1993 rather than at 1990, a tidier number and also the year when Mary Robinson became president. Is Maurice Riordan, born in 1953, more relevant to the Ireland of the 1990s than someone 15 years younger who published a first book in 1992?

Accepting that an element of the arbitrary can never be avoided in making anthologies, let us return to the statement that the anthology collects poets who 'published their first collection after 1993.' Had Anthony Caleshu or Leontia Flynn or Dorothy Molloy or Leanne O'Sullivan been published yet when they were chosen for inclusion? Writers excluded from the anthology will wonder how and why these particular writers-to-be were chosen over others? (The four writers in question are stated to have brought out their first books in 2004). More problematic again are the cases of Nick Laird (whose first collection was published in 2005) and Cathal McCabe (his first book 'as yet unpublished' in 2004). In the seething waters of Irish poetry, this is almost an invitation to the piranhas. Rigorous adherence to stated criteria would have kept them away from the feast. One final swish of the waters: is Michael Murphy, born in Liverpool to an Irish mother, the only new writer of Irish or semi-Irish parentage, born and living outside Ireland, to have been considered for inclusion?

Editors are entitled to their judgements and this review has avoided any listing of writers who might have been included but were not. It is unfortunate, however, that some questionable editorial judgements will have added unnecessarily to the resentment of the excluded and detracted from the positive achievement of the anthology in enabling the reading public to discover some of the diversity of Irish poetry of recent years.

Pickings and Choosings

DENNIS O'DRISCOLL SELECTS RECENT PRONOUNCEMENTS ON POETS AND POETRY

'"Poetic" is usually a compliment; "prosaic" is always an insult.'
– Eric McHenry, *New York Times*, 9 January 2005

'If you can make poetry out of the prose line, that's where you get closest to what we call poetry.'
– Paul Durcan, *The Irish Examiner*, 13 November 2004

'His poetry is generally seen as an extension of his calling as a novelist... The same remarkable qualities that frame his fiction are felt in his poems.'
– James Rother, on John Updike, *Contemporary Poetry Review*, January 2005

'People forget that a poem has to be interesting, just like a piece of journalism has to be interesting, or a novel.'
– Anthony Cronin, *The Irish Times*, 26 November 2004

'Poetry was magic and prose paid the school fees and bills. Any money from poetry was used on antiques, plates, beautiful things; writing prose was treated like a craft.'
– Tomás Graves, on Robert Graves, *The Daily Telegraph*, 1 January 2005

'Poetry requires a kind of exalted indolence, the touch of the gods, pure gift. Prose demands a certain earthbound sobriety, the will of a mule, and *work*.'
– Christian Wiman, *New York Times*, 21 November 2004

'Prose evokes; the well-chosen word describes the thing. But poetry *invokes*; the memorable word conjures its subject from the air.'
– Don Paterson, *T S Eliot Lecture*, October 2004

'Writing prose has a different emotional weight from writing poetry.'
– Stanley Plumly, *American Poetry Review*, January / February 2005

'The short story, like the poem, communicates primarily to the imagination, whereas the novel communicates primarily to the rational mind.'
– Jack Harte, *From Under Gogol's Nose*, 2004

'If poetry was a physical ailment it would more likely be hay fever: sharp, serial, sometimes colourful, not life-threatening. (Novels would be a cluster headache, requiring a dark room and a lie down.)'
– David McCooey, *The Age*, 8 January 2005

'Free from the narrative requirements of fiction or drama, poets can come at their subject from whatever direction language itself will allow. This can cause confusion and headaches all around; it can also, like the charmed words of a magic spell, invite transcendence.'
– Megan Harlan, *San Francisco Chronicle*, 9 January 2005

'All creative writing is storytelling. . . Fiction describes what it means, and poetry becomes what it means in images. Fiction is a linear art made of time, poetry is childishly timeless and circular.'
– Russell Edson, *Double Room*, Spring/Summer 2004

'All these things operate at different levels of my brain. It is like drilling for water... Poetry is the deepest, then right up above that is serious prose, then the charming prose.'
– August Kleinzahler, *The Journal News*, 9 January 2005

'Poets tend to sit by the window while novelists choose the aisle. Novels are social, inclusive, open forms. Poetry has to be a bit more restrictive about the baggage allowance.'
– Nick Laird, *The Irish Times*, 8 January 2005

'A great subject, poetry: but as against what, exactly? There is no prose counterpart to the word "poet" (and no Proser Laureate, no Oxford Professor of Prose)...'
– Christopher Ricks, *Times Literary Supplement*, 23 February 2005

'Poetry makes nothing happen – would that this were true of Religion.'
– Peter Porter, *Afterburner*, 2004

'Poetry makes something happen. The eloquence, the brilliant language, the musical sounds turn out to be going somewhere, toward some discovery or action – sometimes even toward the action of tossing the eloquence or images aside, like a raft that has served its purpose.'
– Robert Pinsky, *The Washington Post*, 13 February 2005

'Good poems resolve emotions; bad ones provoke them.'
– Peter Robinson, *Untitled Deeds*, 2004

'Poetry gives the griever not release from grief but companionship in grief.'
– Donald Hall, *Poetry*, November 2004

'I write because I hope to find some connection between what happens and what I say about it.'
– George Szirtes, *The Poetry Paper*, Winter 2004

'Affirmation of the moment, the place, the here, the now – this is poetry – not the fact of its commercial or non-commercial value or use.'
– John F Deane, *The Irish Times*, 4 January 2005

'A good poem can freeze experience even as it releases and enlarges it, the words utterly intact but ramifying, like a bell that troubles the air long after its sound has stopped.'
– Christian Wiman, *Chicago Tribune*, 19 December 2004

'Perhaps it's because of the mystique surrounding poetry that people think they can knock off a few words and watch them transform, like magic, into something they call a poem.'
– Christina Patterson, *The Independent*, 8 October 2004

'It's difficult to put an opera on, but anyone can get hold of a pen. I think poetry still appeals for that reason.'
– Simon Armitage, *The Times*, 9 October 2004

'If you are a poet, it is a gift... And if you ask where the gift comes from, then I will have to get even more corny and say, maybe it's divine. I think all art is a manifestation of that belief that a gift is a benediction.'
– Derek Walcott, *Wasifari*, Summer 2004

'A special gift isn't bestowed on us by God Almighty, but by another God called Hard Work. I was my own creator.'
– Radmila Lazic, *PN Review*, January / February 2005

'Poetry is a way of mind; the exploration of a tunnel, where blind albino fish seem to float in nostalgic pools of unremembered memory.'
– Russell Edson, *Double Room*, Spring / Summer 2004

'Poetry is a fishing expedition. You don't know what's out there until you start to write.'
– Billy Collins, *Portsmouth Herald*, 23 January 2005

'The best poets seem able both to hook a big one and then throw it back alive.'
– Peter Robinson, *Untitled Deeds*, 2004

'One hallmark of the finest poetry is that no other verse can diminish it, but a peculiar effect of reading deeply in certain enduring work is that for a while one is drawn into thinking that this is the only way poetry should be written.'
– Glyn Maxwell, *The New Republic*, 20 December 2004

'My one axiom in poetry is this: life exceeds art, life exceeds the single poem and the total corpus of poetry. And from that I derive one constant injunction to myself: write always in such a way as to demonstrate the excess of life over the act, the endeavour and the achievement of art.'
– David Constantine, *PBS Bulletin*, Winter 2004

'Rhyme...is a form of relationship and connection, of encounter and metamorphosis... There is something charged and magnetic about a good rhyme, something unsuspected and inevitable, utterly surprising and unforeseen and yet also binding and necessary. It is as if the poet called up the inner yearning for words to find each other.'
– Edward Hirsch, *The Washington Post*, 17 October 2004

'Rhymes throw their weight around too much; they show off...'
– Hugo Williams, *Times Literary Supplement*, 22 October 2004

'Formalism, in itself, is a fetish: specific forms only become interesting when the pressure inside them is on the point of breaking them up.'
– George Szirtes, *PBS Bulletin*, Winter 2004

'Think of [learning poetic forms] as acquiring the tools of your trade, which you may or may not choose to employ. A carpenter doesn't always use a drill, though it would be disastrous for him not to know that it exists for him, and might facilitate what he wants to accomplish.'
– Stephen Dunn, *Smartishpace*, 2004

'I can hardly stand listening to people who say there isn't any good poetry out there. The vitality of the genre stands in total opposition to its paucity of readers, among them people who call themselves poets. It's so obnoxious that attitude of read just yourself or read just the dead.'
– C D Wright, *Here Comes Everybody*, 28 August 2004

'Contemporary poets, alas, have prizes instead of readers. The number of poetry prizes in the land is astonishing.... Such is their plenitude that one is almost inclined to think contemporary poetry less an art than a charity in need of constant donations.'
– Joseph Epstein, *Poetry*, September 2004

'Contemporary poetry can hardly be said to be much on the mind of the general public. The wonder is that so much poetry continues to be written in the face of such resolute indifference.'
– John Barr, *The Poetry Foundation*, September 2004

'Poetry is now so popular that British universities face a supply-and-demand dilemma. So many students want to sign up for poetry classes that there are not enough professional poets to teach them.'
– Shola Adenekan, *Christian Science Monitor*, 30 November 2004

'There aren't a dozen poets writing today who will be read 50 years from now, but there are thousands of people pouring out of MFA programs who think they are entitled to call themselves poets because they have their degrees.'
– August Kleinzahler, *The Journal News*, 9 January 2005

'We're the most important nation on the earth right now, because, one: we have thermonuclear weapons, and two: because we have more talent-ed poets than have ever existed on the face of the earth.'
– Norman Dubie, on the USA, *Poets & Writers*, November/December 2004

'If only poets and novelists could be translated into *musicianhood*, even for a few seconds; then we'd see the vast majority, after only a few notes, revealed as a bunch of desperate scrapers and parpers without a tune in their heads or the rudiments of technique. God, the *time* we would save. . .'
– Don Paterson, *The Book of Shadows*, 2004

'Reading poetry to strangers is a very intimate act. It's kind of like a poetic lap dance.'
– Billeh Nickerson, *The Globe & Mail*, 25 October 2004

'I love being on the road. One night you read to 1,000 people. Next night you change trains three times to get to a little place where you hear a church bell chiming the hour, and walk up the street to the pub and have a fabulous half of ale, and an unusual stranger fetches you to read to 12 people who've prepared a huge buffet, and they are all having affairs with each other's husbands and write verses themselves.'
– Carol Ann Duffy, *The Times*, 16 October 2004

'Three questions that turn bowels to sorbet: / Would you like to try some Japanese whiskey? / Would you like to see my earwax candles? / Would you like to hear my new sestina?'
– Ian Duhig, *The Writer Fellow*, 2004

'We've all been there. Right at the front of that poetry reading where the flannel-trousered bard, half-way through the sixty-seventh section of his Norse epic in pararhymed quatrains, is prefacing the next section with its full progenitive details (Bognor and Lake District), while beyond the darkening windows of the Community Centre gather the glum clouds of late *late* evening, the incipient rumblings of thunder and that thrashing against glass of the first handfuls of hail-seed and rain to wash away any last tatters of hope for your last bus home.'
– Annabel Gage, *Acumen*, January 2005

'For those of us from poorer or working-class backgrounds, the news that you were going to dedicate your life to writing serious verse was received by the community with the same panic as might be your departure for Bader-Meinhof or a transsexual circus.'
– Don Paterson, *New British Poetry*, 2004

'Irony and satire are such a good antidote to oppression because oppression needs to be earnest (or at least look earnest) in order to be feared by those it seeks to cow.'
– Matthew Rohrer, *National Poetry Almanac*, 2 January 2005

'A joke is like an explosion – there's just this little smoke and it's gone. A poem is like a much, much richer joke.'
– Adam Zagajewski, *Agni* online, 2004

'Humor is like a disobedient dog. You call its name and it runs in the other direction.'
– Billy Collins, *New York Times*, 7 October 2004

'The problem with sentimentality is that if it is not risked then the poem can entirely lose emotional register.'
– Caitríona O'Reilly, *Poetry Review*, Autumn 2004

'The whole business of consistency is greatly overemphasised in poetry. Hollandaise sauces should be consistent, but poetry?'
– Conor O'Callaghan, *The Irish Times*, 21 October 2004

'An anthology or selection of poems is...like a spread of cards, the poet dealing out a string of queens, kings and aces, slapping one down after the other in a mood of bravura and triumph.'
– Rosemary Goring, *The Herald*, 25 October 2004

'ALL white space in and around a poem is silence, not paper.'
– Jorie Graham, *Smartishpace*, 2004

'A week is a long time in poetry.'
– Peter Robinson, *Untitled Deeds*, 2004

'I keep saying next time I'm going to write a poem that is only nine lines long, but I think I have an *all you can eat* personality and it doesn't work out.'
– Sydney Lea, *The Writer's Chronicle*, September 2004

'I thought you looked for a dead-end job to support a poet's life... My fantasies were (that) I would be a caretaker of a Civil War cemetery, which didn't have that many visitors, or that I would run a bait shop – something that didn't require a whole lot of maintenance.'
– C D Wright, *News Channel 10*, 29 September 2004

'A poem...is the attire of feeling: the literary form where words seem tailor-made for memory or desire.'
– Carol Ann Duffy, *Out of Fashion*, 2004

'She used every emotional experience as if it were a scrap of material that could be pieced together to make a wonderful dress.'
– Frieda Hughes, on Sylvia Plath, *The Guardian*, 13 November 2004

'Poets do not, on the whole, have a reputation for snappy dressing.'
– Valerie Grove, *The Times*, 16 October 2004

'Poetry expresses the newness of the day.'
– Adam Zagajewski, *Agni* online, 2004

'Writing poetry is my way of celebrating with the world that I have not committed suicide the evening before.'
– Alice Walker, quoted in *The Guardian*, 15 January 2005

'Death is what gets poets up in the morning.'
– Billy Collins, quoted in *San Francisco Chronicle*, 9 January 2005

THE CAT FLAP

Interviewer: . . .*What do you read at present?*

The latest book I've discovered is the great dictionary of the Customs Administration that we owe to an edict of Vincent Auriol, then Minister of Finance. It is entitled *Répertoire générale du tarif* and appeared in 1937. Two quarto volumes. Weight fifty kilos. I take them every place with me because I'm going to need them some day soon when I begin to write *La Carissima*, the mystical life of Mary Magdalene, the only woman who made Christ weep.

Interviewer: *You need the customs tariffs in order to write that book?*

My dear sir, it's a matter of language. For several years, each time that I prepare to write a book, I first arrange the vocabulary I am going to employ. Thus for *L'Homme foudroyé*, I had a list of three thousand words arranged in advance, and I used all of them. That saved me a lot of time and gave a certain lightness to my work. It was the first time I used that system. I don't know how I happened on to it. . . It's a question of language. Language is a thing that seduced me. Language is a thing that perverted me. Language is a thing that formed me. Language is a thing that deformed me. That's why I am a poet, probably because I am very sensitive to the language – correct or incorrect, I wink at that. I ignore and despise grammar, which is at the point of death, but I am a great reader of dictionaries and if my spelling is none too sure it's because I am too attentive to the pronunciation, this idiosyncrasy of the living language. In the beginning was not the word, but the phrase, a modulation. Listen to the song of birds!

The above useful advice and observations, from Blaise Cendrars, in conversation with Michel Manoll in 1950, was gleaned by The Cat Flap on his journey through the *Paris Review* archives online. The idea of arranging vocabulary in advance is eminently sensible and time-saving and could, possibly, with so many calls on a poet's time, even be outsourced. The Cat Flap is currently considering the establishment of a small but dedicated company devoted to the advance preparation of vocabulary for writers. Reasonable terms assured. Discounts for any vocabulary not used, or a credit note towards the purchase of future vocabularies.

'The DNA of literature', the *Paris Review*'s project to put 'over 50 years of literary wisdom rolled up in 300+ Writers-at-Work interviews online free' is now up to the Sixties, so you can grab Jean Cocteau ('Appreciation of art is a moral erection; otherwise mere dilettantism. I believe sexuality is the basis of all friendship'), Robert Graves, Allen Ginsberg, Robert Lowell, Marianne Moore, Ezra Pound, William Carlos Williams or Vladimir Nabokov ('I am as American as April in Arizona.

The flora, the fauna, the air of the western states, are my links with
Asiatic and Arctic Russia.') If you want to read Dennis O'Driscoll's
extensive interview with Les Murray in the forthcoming print edition of
the *Paris Review* (Spring 2005), you'll need to buy it, as it will be some
years before it's archived on the site.

*

'Listen to the song of birds!' said Cendrars, but listening to the songs of
birds is, according to Jane Yeh in *Poetry Review* (Winter, 2004), strictly for
the birds. 'For some reason, all the poetry I've been paid to read lately
has been about nature. (Who knew so many poets were living in the
countryside?) As someone who has never seen a hedgerow in real life,
and who can't tell the difference between a chaffinch and a thrush, I have
to take it on trust that these things are worth writing about.' Yeh is
bothered by the sheer amount of nature she is expected to deal with in
her reviews of English poetry, which must indeed be a burden to her.
The Cat Flap for his part feels that urban poets should, every now and
then, be taken on field excursions to the countryside where, for a small
consideration, instruction could be given on, for instance, hedgerows
(those fortunate enough not to have been bulldozed to make way for a
prairie) and crucial differences between chaffinches (reddish-brown
plumage in the male, blue-grey crown and nape, greenish-brown back,
heavy bill, white wing markings, the female altogether plainer and
lacking red plumage) and thrushes (brown above and cream coloured
below with dark spots and chevrons, melodic song). Likewise poets from
the country might profitably be introduced (perhaps even by Jane) to tall
buildings, trams, kebabs, bicycle lanes, gur cakes, coddle, rounded off by
a *latte* in the Clarence and tickets for Shels v. Bohemians.

*

A note comes in the electronic letterbox announcing that the Arts
Sections and County Development Boards of Laois, Offaly, Longford and
Westmeath are creating a six-month collaborative creative writing
project for young people. The chosen writer, who will need a fast car,
will work with groups throughout the four counties. Compared to some
other places, residencies for writers in Ireland are few and far between. In
England the art has been considerably refined, and there is hardly a chip
shop or factory that doesn't have its earnest resident poet doing his or
her bit for the economy. Christina Patterson, former director of the
Poetry Society in England, and indeed former organiser of Poetry Places,
the society's programme of residencies, subjected poems produced
during some of them to close scrutiny in the *Independent*, of which she is
now deputy literary editor. First was Roddy Lumsden, poet in residence
at St Andrew's Bay Golf Resort and Spa, whose poem 'Hotel Showers of

the World' was judged to pass muster (or water); Sarah Wardle, the poet in residence at Tottenham Hotspur Football Club, and an ardent Spurs fan, got the nod for her poem 'At White Hart Lane', but Patterson was underwhelmed by the poem produced by Maria Garner, the poet in residence to Beacon Hill Allotments, Cleethorpes ('The earth smells of new potatoes / Sweet peas caress the night with their scent / Roses and honeysuckle do not compete / Each knows its own beauty.'), and by the poem Ian McMillan produced during a spell as poet in residence at Humberside Police. All of the poems were conscientious responses by the poets to their residencies, which presumably had clauses requiring the poets to contribute socially useful poems. The Cat Flap is deeply in favour of schemes which allow poets to buy some time to write and promote poetry while they are at it, but isn't there a danger that all these attempts to make poets and poetry useful merely betray a fear of or indifference to what both might get up to if left to their own devices, or assume poetry is fundamentally a social art, a minor branch of public service; that sociability, an interest in education and general all round affability are part of the poet's make-up? Don't poets get tired of bending over backwards to show how caring they are, how they can contribute to effective policing or gardening or education or recycling or communication strategies? Does all patronage need to be so instrumental, product-driven, outcome-oriented (as we say in the arts)? What about a bit of loafing and soul-inviting? Residencies for the disgruntled, the unsocialised, the permanently solitary, or which go in fear of the anthology, the CD, the website, the school visit. Or residencies where the poet is paid to avoid the production of poetry altogether, to sit silently for six months in a well-stocked library with a modest stipend and a couple of cases of burgundy. The Cat Flap announces his availability. . .

*

Translation is in the air. This issue contains poetry in translation by Elizabeth Mac Donald, David Butler, Mary O'Donnell, Alice Lyons and Justyn Hunia. The winter edition of the *Poetry Review* (London) is a special translation issue, with an essay by Sarah Maguire, founder of the recently established Poetry Translation Centre in London, whose workshops focus on 'the delicate art of how best to produce translations that work successfully as poems in English whilst retaining a close relationship to the original poem.' You can see the process at work at **www.poetrytranslation.soas.ac.uk/** Cork 2005 is presenting a series of events and books of translations by Cork poets of poets from Europe, while Ciaran Carson's translation of *Cúirt an Mheán Oíche* will be launched at this year's Cúirt. As always when poetry translation is undertaken, the great ancient questions and dusted off and paraded. Should the poet speak the language? How faithful is faithful? To what extent should the original be domesticated or naturalised in the target language? When is a translation not a translation but another creature entirely? Should the translation of poetry be left to poets? Do poets only translate into themselves? When you take away the language, what are you left with? How should translation be presented to the public? In a recent *Poetry Ireland News*, David Butler feels so strongly that all translations should have the original on the facing page 'that when I come across a mono-lingual book of translations which rhyme my first instinct is to reach for the bin', since 'it is seldom indeed that equivalent rhyme scheme can be set up in English without doing a good deal of violence to the original.' The recent Faber anthologies of French and Italian poetry are likely to suffer that fate, since both are monolingual, leaving it to the reader to take the work on trust, though the distance between original and translation can be, em, interesting. There is a long tradition in English of interventionist translation – one of the joys of world domination – where the originals are deployed as springboards for poetic elaboration, invention or gleeful appropriation.

> Who can say to the birds
> *shut the fuck up*
> or tell the sheep in the yow trummle
> not to struggle and leap?

This is how Goethe ('Wer kann gebieten den Vögeln / Still zu sein auf der Flur?') sounds in Tom Paulin's *The Road To Inver* (Faber, 2004), 'verse translations' of European poetry, 'the richest collection of its kind since Robert Lowell's *Imitations*.' The Lowell reference is a studied signal of the poems' fairly distant relationships with their originals; the book is a kind of translation by free association, variations on a theme suggested by an original or someone else's translation of an original, or, sometimes, a game whose point is to lurch as far as possible from the original: 'Henry Snodden and me we've nearly forgotten / that scraggy coastguard station – / a ruin from the Black and Tan war / it stood on Tim Ring's hill above the harbour...' (Montale, 'The Coastguard Station'). We might be in danger of bewilderment if this were the only kind of 'translation' we encountered, but if we want the impassioned relationship with the original scrupulously reconstructed in the host language we can always turn to Hölderlin in the English of Michael Hamburger or David Constantine or Christopher Middleton, or to Hamburger's or John Felstiner's Celan. The spectrum of possible responses is as vast as the dis-tance between 'La casa dei doganieri' and Henry Snodden's scraggy wee coastguard station. . .

Notes on Contributors

Gary Allen's second collection, *Exile*, is published by Black Mountain Press. A collection of short stories is forthcoming from Lagan Press.

Margaret Atwood's selected poems, *Eating Fire* is published by Virago. Her many awards as a novelist include the Booker Prize in 2000 for *The Blind Assassin*.

Ingeborg Bachmann: see Mary O'Donnell's essay in this issue.

Michael S Begnal was editor of the Galway-based literary magazine *The Burning Bush*. His collection, *Ancestor Worship*, will be published this year by Salmon. He has appeared in numerous journals, and in anthologies such as *Breaking the Skin: New Irish Poetry* (Black Mountain Press, 2002) and *Go Nuige Seo* (Coiscéim, 2004).

David Butler's translations of Pessoa, *Selected Pessoa*, was published by Dedalus in 2004, while a collection of his own work, *Via crucis* is forthcoming, also from Dedalus. He is the winner of the English-language category in this year's Féile Filíochata Poetry Competition.

Louise C Callaghan's first collection of poetry was *The Puzzle-Heart*, (Salmon, 1999). She edited the anthology *Forgotten Light: Memory Poems* (A & A Farmar, 2003), gathering an array of Irish and international poets. *Remember the Birds* is forthcoming from Salmon in 2005.

Declan Collinge has published four collections, two in Irish and two in English; his most recent collection, *Common Ground*, was published by Inisfail Press. He is the author of the popular 'Saibhreas' series of Irish-language textbooks.

Gerald Dawe has published six collections of poetry, including *The Morning Train* (1999) and *Lake Geneva* (2003), both from Gallery. *The Night Fountain: Uncollected Poems of Salvatore Quasimodo*, translated with Marco Sonzogni, is forthcoming from Arc.

Andrew Fitzsimons is editor of the *Journal of Irish Studies*.

Naomi Foyle is a British-Canadian poet living in Brighton. Her most recent pamphlet, *Canada*, was published by Echo Room Press in 2004. She is editor of the posthumous *Selected Works of Martin Crawford*, forthcoming from Lagan Press.

Lavinia Greenlaw's third colllection *Minsk* (Faber, 2003) was nominated for the Forward, Whitbread and TS Eliot prizes in 2003.

Eamon Grennan's most recent collection is *The Quick of It* (Gallery, 2004).

Justyn Hunia is a translator and musician. Between 1997-2003 he was co-founder of an *avant-garde* jazz-rock group, Gargantua, in Kraków, Poland. He studied English and translation at the Jagiellonian University, Kraków. He has translated into Polish the poetry of Liz Lochhead, Eavan Boland, Cathal McCabe, Carolyn Forché and Alice Lyons, among others.

I measc na leabhar filíochta atá foilsithe ag **Biddy Jenkinson** le Coiscéim tá *Baisteadh Gintlí* (1986), *Dán na hUidhre* (1991), *Amhras Neimhe* (1997) agus *Rogha Dánta* (2000).Tá bailiúchán nua dá cuid, *Sna Sranna Ceoil*, á ullmhú ag Coiscéim.

Fred Johnston is founder of The Western Writers' Centre. A novella, *Tracé de Dieu*, was published by Wynkin de worde in 2003, while *Being Anywhere: New and selected Poems* was published by Lagan in 2002.

John Kinsella's *Peripheral Vision: New and Selected Poems* was published by Norton in 2003; Norton will also publish *The New Arcadia*, in 2005.

Thomas Kinsella was born in Dublin in 1928. His *Collected Poems*, published by Oxford University Press, appeared in 1996, and was reprinted by Carcanet in 2002. He has translated extensively from Irish. Peppercanister will publish *Marginal Economy* this year.

Mario Luzi: see Elizabeth Mac Donald's essay in this issue.

Alice Lyons was born in Paterson, New Jersey and now lives in County Roscommon. She is the recipient of the inaugural Ireland Chair of Poetry Bursary and the Patrick Kavanagh Award.

Aifric Mac Aodha is a post-graduate student in The Department of Modern Irish, UCD. She also works as an occasional lecturer in the Department of Early-Irish. Her work has been published in *Poetry Ireland Review*, *Innti*, *Bliainiris*, *Comhar* and *Feasta*.

Elizabeth Mac Donald teaches English at Pisa University. She completed the M.Phil. in Creative Writing at Trinity College, Dublin and is working on a novel.

Tom Mac Intyre was born in Cavan in 1931. A dual-language writer, he has written poetry and prose as well as many plays for the Abbey Theatre (Peacock Stage), including *The Great Hunger* (1983-6), which toured internationally, and his version of *Cúirt An Mhean Oiche/The Midnight Court* (1999). His poetry collections include *Fleur-du-Lit* (Dedalus, 1994), and *Stories of the Wandering Mohn* (Lilliput Press, 2000). He is a member of Aosdána, and lives in Co Cavan.

Eugene McCabe was born in Glasgow in 1930 of Irish parents. A playwright, novelist, short-fiction writer and poet, his most recent book of stories is *Heaven Lies About Us* (London, Cape, 2005). He lives in Monaghan.

John Montague's *Collected Poems* (Gallery Press) appeared in 1995, the year he received the America Ireland Fund Literary Award. He became the first Ireland Professor of Poetry in 1998, while his most recent collection is *Drunken Sailor* (Gallery Press, 2004).

Alan Jude Moore read as part of the Poetry Ireland Introductions Series of Readings in 2001. His first collection, *Black State Cars*, won the Salmon Poetry Publication Prize and was published by Salmon in 2004.

Gerry Murphy's fifth collection, *Torso of an Ex-Girlfriend*, was published by Dedalus in 2002. He was born and lives in Cork City.

Hugh O'Donnell is a frequent contributor to *Poetry Ireland Review*, as well as being widely published elsewhere.

John O'Donnell has published two collections, *Some Other Country* (Bradshaw, 2002) and *Icarus Sees His Father Fly* (Dedalus, 2004).

Mary O'Donnell's fourth collection, *September Elegies*, was published by Lapwing in 2003. She is also a novelist and a member of Aosdána.

Dennis O'Driscoll's *New and Selected Poems* (Anvil Press), a poetry Book Society Commendation, was published last year. Publications in 2005 will include a prose-poem chapbook, *50 O'clock* (Happy Dragons Press, UK), poems in *The Wake Forest Series of Irish Poetry* 1 (Wake Forest University Press, USA), and his *Paris Review* interview with Les Murray.

Alexandre O'Neill: see David Butler's essay in this issue.

Barra Ó Seaghdha is a teacher, editor and critic. He lives in Dublin.

Peter Robinson was born in England in 1953. Since 1989 he has taught and lived in Japan. His *Selected Poems* was published in 2003 by Carcanet.

Mike Shields was born in Jarrow, England in 1938. A former editor of *Here Now* and *ORBIS*, his poems and translations have appeared widely.

Cherry Smyth's first collection, *When the Lights Go Up*, was published by Lagan Press in 2001. She has edited an anthology of women prisoners' writing, *A Strong Voice in a Small Place*, which won the Raymond Williams Community Publishing Award in 2003.

Gerard Smyth has been publishing poetry in literary journals in Ireland, Britain and North America since the late 1960s. He is the author of five collections, the latest being *Daytime Sleeper* (2002), and *A New Tenancy*, (2004), both published by Dedalus.

Wislawa Szymborska received the Nobel Prize for Literature in 1996.

Susan Wicks's most recent collection, *Night Toad: New and Selected Poems* (Bloodaxe, 2003), was a Poetry Book Society Recommendation. She directs the Creative Writing programme at the University of Kent.

C K Williams's most recent collection, *The Singing*, won the National Book Award of the USA. He has previously won both the Pulitzer Prize and the PEN Award for his poetry.

Charles Wright's books include *Buffalo Yoga* (2004), *Negative Blue* (2000), *Black Zodiac* (1997), which won the Pulitzer Prize and the Los Angeles Times Book Prize, and his translation of Eugenio Montale's *The Storm and Other Poems* (1978), which was awarded the PEN Translation Prize. He is Souder Family Professor of English at the University of Virginia in Charlottesville.